I0200031

COLLECTED WORKS
OF
C.R. LAMA

COLLECTED WORKS
OF
C.R. LAMA

COMPILED AND EDITED
BY
JAMES LOW

Published by Simply Being www.simplybeing.co.uk

© James Low, 2013

The right of JAMES LOW to be identified as the author of this work has been asserted by him in accordance with the Copyright, Designs and Patents Act, 1988.

All Rights Reserved. No part of this book may be printed, reproduced or utilised in any form or by electronic, mechanical or other means, now known or hereafter invented, including photocopying and recording, or in any information storage retrieval system, without prior permission in writing from the author.

Your support of the author's rights is appreciated.

British Library Cataloguing in Publication Data. A catalogue record for this book is available from the British Library.

ISBN: 978-0-9569239-2-9

Typeset in Tibetan unicode font: Jomolhari-ID-a3d.ttf; headings: Avenir; body of text: Palatino Linotype; transliteration from Tibetan: Arial; Translation lines: Times New Roman, Palatino Linotype, Book Antiqua.

*May all beings awaken
to the infinite depth and light
which is the ground of their being*

Contents

Preface   *ix*
Introduction   *xi*

1. Vajrayāna in Tibet   1

2. The Nyingma Tradition   19

3. Bardo Instructions Radiating Clarity like the Sun   35

4. The Root Verses of the Bardos   55

5. Vajrasattva Meditation Purifying All Errors and
   Obscurations   65

6. Padmasambhava Introduces Himself   77

7. Padmasambhava: Meaningful to Behold   83

8. Padmasambhava's Predictions   89

9. Extracts from Prefaces   107

10. Brief Teachings   113

11. Khordong Monastery   135

12. Education in Khordong Monastery   145

13. Khordong Monastery: Annual Cycle of Rituals   151

14. New Year Celebrations   167

15. Comments on Culture   173

16. Rigdzin Godem and Sikkim   181

Bibliography   187

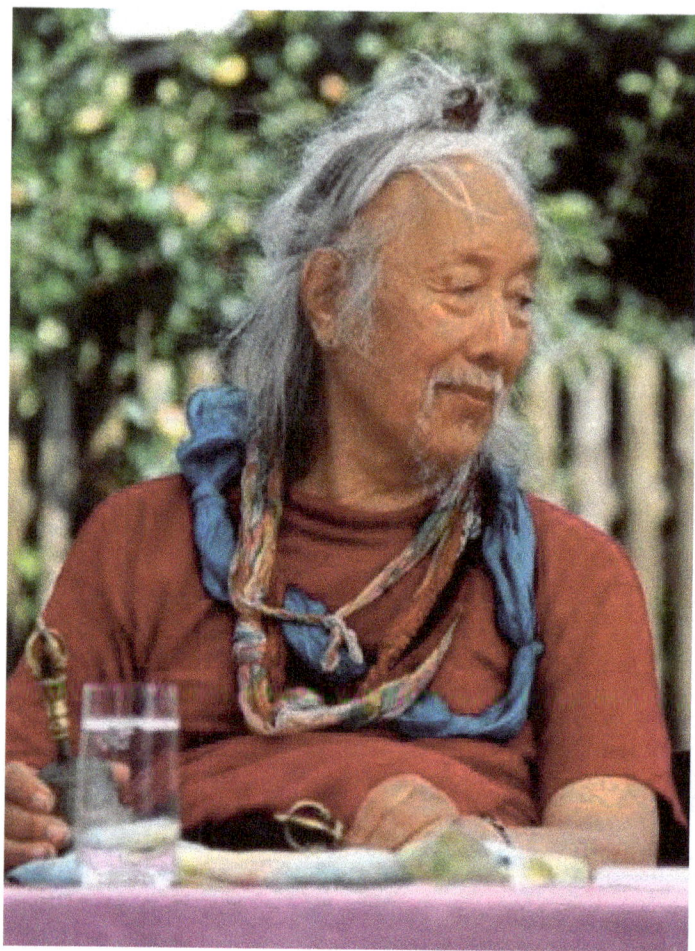

May the sunshine of the teacher's smile and the rainfall of enriching instruction cause all seeds of enlightenment to sprout and flourish in the ten directions

Preface

The production of this book has been a labour of love. The original texts from which it has been prepared were often in a very poor state of grammar, semantics and accuracy of details so a great deal of checking and revising has been required. Yet it has not seemed a burden as the work brought my colleague, Barbara Terris, and myself back to the feeling tone of our early work with Rinpoche in India.

As the Buddhist texts remind us again and again, no progress can be made without open-hearted faith. To find a teacher worthy of that is truly a rare and precious opportunity. The opening of the heart allows the stream of blessing and transmission to flow in, and this is the basis of the continuity of the tradition. Devotion also opens the heart to the beauty of the moment, however it is. Devotion frees us from reification, objectification and judgement, the three tendencies which make our world and our hearts so dense and heavy.

The typing and retyping of the texts was done by Barbara Terris. Barbara checked over the work for Sanskrit and Tibetan spellings. Our thanks to Gyurme Dorje for his help with this. Sarah Allen prepared the final version for publishing.

We hope the book will interest those who have a connection with C.R. Lama and also those who are interested in the diverse topics covered in this small volume.

James Low

If there is some merit in this work, may it help all beings awaken.
If there is no merit, may its emptiness protect all beings from disturbance

Introduction

This book presents a wide range of short works that C.R. Lama engaged with over his years as Reader in Indo-Tibetan Studies at Visva-Bharati University, Santiniketan, West Bengal. Some are translations, some are original writings and some are brief teachings which he gave while working on other texts. The aim of the volume is to give a glimpse of the range of interests and styles of one of the first Lamas to freely communicate with the modern world.

C.R. Lama

While living in India he introduced himself as C.R. Lama and Indians generally addressed him as Lamaji. Among Tibetan people he was known as Khordong Terchen Tulku Chimed Rigdzin (*'Khor-gDong gTer-Chen sPrul-sKu 'Chi-Med Rig-'Dzin*) and addressed as Rinpoche.

He was born in 1922 on the full moon day of the 10th month. He was recognised as the third incarnation of Khordong Terchen Drophan Lingpa Drolo Tsal (*'Khor-gDong gTer-Chen 'Gro-Phan gLing-Pa Gro-Lod rTsal*) by Tulku Tshultrim Zangpo (*sPrul-sKu Tshul-Khrims bZang-Po*) whom Rinpoche always referred to as Tulku Tsorlo (*sPrul-sKu Tshul-Lo*) and who later became his main teacher. He was also recognised as the incarnation of the Body of Khyeu-Chung Lotsawa (*Khye'u-Chung Lo-Tsa-Ba*), the Speech of Nanam Dorje Dudjom (*sNa-Nam rDo-rJe bDud-'Joms*) and the Mind of Padmasambhava. At the age of four he was enthroned as the head of Khordong Monastery (*'Khor-gDong dGon-Pa*) and its eleven principle sub-monasteries. As he often recounted, he then commenced an intense education where he had to demonstrate greater capacity in all areas than the other students. As an example of the way selfish motives could have a good outcome, he explained that the status of the monastery depended on the qualities of its head. If the head lama was famous for power and learning then many offerings would be received – so other people's interest in his education he likened to fattening up a calf for a feast. *"Although I was beaten and pressured I am now glad for I learned many things that have made me useful to others."*

At the age of ten he travelled to central Tibet and studied for two years under Nyamnyi Dorje (*mNyam-Nyid rDo-rJe*), the head of the principal Jangter (*Byang-gTer*) Monastery of Dorje Drag (*rDo-rJe Brag*). He returned to Khordong as the official Jangter lineage holder for East Tibet. He continued his studies under Tulku Tsorlo of Shugchung Gonpa (*Shug-Chung dGon-Pa*), a monastery famous for its careful and disciplined performance of rituals and religious dances. He became proficient in all aspects of ritual and practice and at seventeen was tested on his skills and awarded the title of Dorje Lopon Chenpo (*rDo-rJe sLob-dPon Chen-Po*), signifying mastery in all aspects of tantric practice.

Tulku Tsorlo then made seven predictions to guide him in the future. He told C.R. Lama,

"At eighteen you must leave the monastery without telling anyone you're going and then make extensive pilgrimage in the border areas of Bhutan, Sikkim and Nepal. You must marry a woman from Sikkim for this will ensure your long life. You must make a three-year retreat at Tsho Pema and not defend yourself when you are robbed. You will fly in the sky at the age of thirty-seven. When you are near sixty your eyesight will weaken and you must act to preserve it for your further Dharma activities. After this you must return to Khordong and give all the necessary teachings and initiations. You will live to eighty-four or to one hundred and twenty years depending on circumstances."

He duly left his monastery at 11 p.m. on the full moon night of the first month of the earth rabbit year, 1939, with two attendants. He left a message to say that he was leaving and was not to be followed. He went to Lhasa and worked for sometime in the Dalai Lama's administration, sorting out historical documents and arranging the library. Then he went to India via Bhutan and Sikkim. This was before the Chinese invasion and the border was easy to cross. He lived in Kalimpong for some years, married a Sikkimese woman and, through her uncle, did some work in the border area near Tawang for the newly independent Indian government.

Dudjom Rinpoche encouraged him to become head of the Nyingma Monastery at Tsho Pema (mTsho-Padma) but C.R. Lama declined saying that monasteries mean sponsors and sponsors mean trouble. Because he wanted to start a family, he focused on getting a secure job and, using his intuition, intelligence and political connections, he secured the post of Lecturer and then of Reader in Indo-Tibetan studies at Visva-Bharati University, Santiniketan. He had already acquired a good working knowledge of Nepali and Hindi and now focused on learning Bengali and Sanskrit. His early years of disciplined endeavour made this an easy task and he was soon working with Indian scholars on the reconstruction of early Bengali and Hindi Buddhist texts that had been lost in India but were preserved in the Tibetan language from work done during the Second Translation period around the 11 century AD.

He became a familiar figure on the Indian University conference circuit, again and again illustrating the importance of Buddhist learning as a means to understand Indian culture. He also taught Tibetan language at Calcutta University for many years.

At the age of thirty-seven he went to Italy to work with Giuseppe Tucci in Rome and to Munich in Germany to work with Professor Hoffmann. This exposure to European culture in the late 1950's gave him the sense of the intense energy that western people devoted to worldly existence. He said that seeing how enthusiastic they were to get lost, he had no interest in western culture.

C.R. Lama worked at Visva-Bharati University until his retirement and for some of this period Tulku Thondup Rinpoche was his close colleague. Rinpoche lived in a university house together with his wife, Sangye Dolma, known to all as Amala, and their five children. The house had a verandah, an enclosed yard, a garden and several outbuildings. In the 1970s and early 1980s it became a hive of activity as a few western people settled around him. At times it was like the Tower of Babel with Bengali, Nepali, Hindi, Tibetan, English, French, German and Dutch being spoken in attempts at cross-cultural communication. C.R. Lama did little formal Dharma teaching. He did not enjoy teaching or giving explanations. He taught by creating situations where direct experience collapsed conceptual expectations. He rarely talked about his own life and when he did the accounts he gave often differed. He emphasised that the accumulation of 'facts' leads to an unhelpful false sense of certainty. *"Everything is stories, everything is illusion. Only emptiness is true."*

The number of western students present at any one time varied from one to ten and all were encouraged to engage in some way with the preparation of translations of ritual texts. These texts were presented with the original Tibetan and the word and sentence meaning in English. [*See*, the Chapter 4, *The Root Verses of the Bardos* for an example.] Many thousands of pages were prepared in this way by typing and handwriting on waxed paper which were then printed off on Rinpoche's Gestetner machine using inked drums. There was a sense of great pressure all the time, a mood of intensity and urgency and long hours were worked every day and often into the night relying on a carbide lamp or candle light. It was common for the texts to be printed and the many pages sorted just before the initiation or practice was due to start. There was the sense of living in a field of ceaseless unpredictable energy, the mandala of Senge Dongma (*Seng-Ge gDong-Ma*), one of Rinpoche's main practices.

On the 10th and 25th days of the Tibetan lunar month we all participated in rituals wearing our red dharma robes. These pujas had great power and focus as Rinpoche opened himself fully to the rather clouded potentials of his students. The sun of his awareness was able to burn some gaps in these clouds and bring the immediacy of presence out of the pages of the ritual texts and into the lives of those who surrounded him. An example of such a ritual can be found in BEING GURU RINPOCHE [1].

The mood in his house was often wild, like a storm, like a threat, like an explosion. There was no chance of complacency, for attention to detail and precision of intention were the only factors keeping the intensity focused. When this went wrong, there was shouting, banging, gloom, silence and then terror, like a monsoon storm. These moods could last for days offering a chance – but only a chance – of seeing the empty nature of fear. Without practice the situation was intolerable.

When I met C.R. Lama for the first time he said, *"The Buddha is not a nice man."* The fantasy of sweetness, safety and calm was one that he was happy to dissolve. His aim was *dis*-illusionment – offering a collapsing of assumptions, hopes and fears, intentions and plans.

When students were clinging to these frames of reference *dis*-illusion-ment was painful and a source of dismay. Again and again he showed the specificity of the moment, the discovery of whether one's 'share' (*Rang-Chas*), one's luck, was to be found in his mandala or not. Fit, conjunction, connection – this is the opening to what is here. If there is no fit, the transmission does not occur. It is up-front and personal with nowhere to hide and no chance to pretend.

By the time C.R. Lama retired his children had left home so he and his wife left Santiniketan and moved to Siliguri in North Bengal, where the hills meet the plains. From there he made many visits to Europe and gradually attracted a large following of those who participated in the rituals and experienced the openness of his presence. At this stage in his life his mood was more peaceful and, though occasionally direct and challenging, his benign presence offered a sense of direc-tion and reassurance to the mainly young people who came seeking to find a meaning for their lives.

His final years were spent building a monastery at Siliguri in order to provide a base for the continuity of the monastic side of his lineage. The lineage continues in Europe in a variety of settings and in a low-key manner.

I lived in a room at the back of his house for eight years and my own experience of Rinpoche during that time was incredibly varied. It is impossible to sum him up or even to give a clear account of how he was, since he was whatever he was in the moment, without shame or fear. He was not trying to project an image nor working to make people like him and this offered others infinite freedom. You could make of him what you would – but was that an insight into him or merely a projection of one's own interpretive matrix?

When I first went with my friend Barbara to Santiniketan to study Tibetan with C.R. Lama, he and his family were away and an American Kagyu monk, Tsultrim, was looking after his house. We left our bags on a wooden bed frame on the locked verandah and went out to eat. By the time we returned our bags were in the courtyard under the standpipe getting soaking wet. Right from the beginning he was indi-cating that, "*You have to rely on me, but don't rely on me.*" As he often said of himself, "*I am liar number one, cheater number one*", and, "*I don't trust anyone and number one, I don't trust myself.*" The only true refuge is one's own mind and that is a treacherous terrain full of illusory certainty.

When I started to work on Tibetan texts with C.R. Lama, I would prepare the text as well as I could and then he would go through it with what he called his 'running system', giving the meaning of difficult words and phrases as quickly as he could. He would say, *"Quick is good"* and describe how as a child his writing went across the slate like a bird crossing the sky. Soon the main thing he said was, *"You know this"* and leap ahead. It was painful and confusing to see that he had more faith in me that I had in him. Whenever I got lost in relationships or drinking or rebellious moods he would tell me that this was due to other people's negative energy and not to worry.

The vast range of his knowledge and skills was amazing and he could turn his hand to any activity. When I was preparing to go on a traveling retreat in Ladakh and needed a tent he told me to go to the market and buy so many metres of white cotton, of a kind used in India to wrap parcels for the post. When I returned he had called a local tailor who was there on the verandah with his sewing machine. Rinpoche measured the cloth by his arm-span and tore it into ten pieces and directed the tailor on how to sew. Within a few hours my tent was ready and already invested with his protective energy.

When we went on pilgrimage to Tsho Pema he noticed that the floating islands in the sacred lake were not moving. He told the Abbot of the Nyingma Monastery there that this was a bad sign and that they should be encouraged to float about. He told me to swim out to them and push them free so that they could travel with the breeze as the traditional texts described. The local people were very unhappy but he began chanting in his powerful beautiful voice and gradually all the small islands, which are lumps of roots and earth and reeds, started to move. So many times he acted directly into the situation and dealt with the consequences without hesitation or embarrassment. He was confident and clear, manifesting a huge impact and then, in an instant, being invisible.

He would often go to his office in the university wearing a singlet and lunghi, the clothing of the rickshaw men. His wife would complain and ask him, *"Have you no dignity? What will people say?"*. He would reply, *"Well, when they see me coming do you think they say, 'This is C.R. Lama coming' or do they say, 'This is C.R. Lama's clothes coming'?"*

His main method of transmission was through the intensity of ritual practice. His first incarnation had travelled to Zangdopalri (*Zangs-mDog dPal-Ri*) on a goose and spent three days there with Padmasambhava. Rinpoche told us that the attendants of Nuden Dorje wondered if he had died because his body did not move, but then he returned with many teachings. Rinpoche said that the purpose of our rituals was to actually see Padmasambhava and to gain teaching from him. This was not a metaphor or an 'as if' situation – it was 'as is'. And so we prayed with one-pointed intensity while Rinpoche used all his meditation power, his voice, and his skills with cymbals and drum to bring Padmasambhava into a living relationship with this small group of devotees. The main point is direct experience, not theory, not knowledge, but the actual experience of one's own nature as openness, clarity and ceaseless participation.

Rinpoche was impatient with restrictive structures, with pomposity, and he was highly antagonistic when he saw Dharma being used as a means to secure worldly ends. Who can say who he was? Certainly a trickster, certainly a terton, certainly a shining force for good, who pointed to the heart of the practice. As he often told me, *"Other lamas hope to die with mantras on their lips, but I want to die with my mouth full of delicious milky sweets."*

The Texts

The first two chapters, *Vajrayāna in Tibet and The Nyingma Tradition* are texts written in Tibetan by C.R. Lama. They have many similarities in their content and this repetition underlines the traditional importance ascribed to gaining a clear overview of how the various styles and levels of practice fit together. Unfortunately the Tibetan originals have been lost, eaten by termites. The first two texts contain many Buddhist technical terms and these are given in English, Sanskrit and Tibetan. C.R. Lama was insistent that terms be given in their original language for there the meaning has been clearly established, whereas in English and other European languages the meanings of the terms are still not defined, being approximations and part of a work in progress. These two texts establish the background of the practice by pointing to the historical development of the specific Nyingma orientation. The Nyingma 'school' comprises a loose collection of groups of people following the teachings arising from Padmasambhava who in the eighth century AD established tantric Buddhism to Tibet.

There are many Dharma paths and in the West one can now easily visit different Dharma centres presenting teachings that have had no direct contact with each other for 1000 years. How to choose what is right for us? Well, perhaps we are as much 'chosen' as 'choosing'; our lives are revealed to us as we find ourselves been drawn to someone, or to some path because it takes our fancy. The manifesting of our connection with the Dharma is rarely reason-led, rather we are taken with and by some image, voice or idea and we find, perhaps without knowing why, that we are on the path. Yet this is not a mere whim, and some knowledge of the rich history of the tradition can strengthen our sense of belonging – a vital feeling if we are to continue for months, years and lifetimes.

Chapter 1, *Vajrayana in Tibet*, gives a brief description of how tantric teaching came to be known to human beings. It was not the result of a person having an interesting idea and then developing a system from that. Rather it is a lineage present from the beginning of time and passed on through beings existing in diverse forms in diverse realms. The unbroken lineage proceeding from its 'divine' or natural origin parallels its teaching of the unbroken continuity between all phenomena and between these phenomena and their natural source or ground. Further details of the early history of these teachings can be found in THE NYINGMA SCHOOL OF TIBETAN BUDDHISM: ITS FUNDAMENTALS AND HISTORY [2]. This chapter also sets out the structure of the levels of tantric practice and points to important differences of view and meditation between them.

Chapter 2, *The Nyingma Tradition*, extends the material set out in Chapter 1 by giving a clear account of how the way we view our situation generates patterns of embodied response. As long as we believe that subject and object are truly separate and intrinsically real, each with their own defining essence or inherent self-nature, then we are condemned to a long, slow, hard path of purification and development on which we encounter many obstacles. The main obstacle is, in fact, our own belief in our existence as a separate entity.

This chapter points to the vital importance of opening to, and abiding within, the non-dual view of Dzogchen, the pinnacle of the Buddha's teaching. This view introduces us to the natural perfection of our own current situation so that without making any external or internal changes we awaken to our primordial buddhahood, the non-duality of the intrinsic purity of unborn openness and the clarity of spontaneous manifestation. This is the teaching that C.R. Lama embodied and expressed in the carefree immediacy of his participation in all that he encountered.

Chapters 3, *Bardo Instructions Radiating Clarity like the Sun*, and 4, *The Root Verses of the Bardos*, focus on the experience of the bardos, the in-between or intermediate states. Chapter 3 is part of the terma (*gTer-Ma, treasure*) collection of C.R. Lama's first incarnation. Chapter 4 is part of the KARMA LINGPA ZHITRO cycle. Our lives are nothing but experience, ungraspable experience; whatever we grasp at is just another form of experience, present only as we attend to it. Rather than asserting definite stages to our lives, stages that we will occupy and master, the teachings on the bardo point to the transitional and contingent nature of every moment of our unfolding. We are always between what is gone and what is yet to come – life consists of moments not things. These teachings encourage us to fully open to the moment we are in. If we are fully open and receive the fullness of the moment we will be full and empty at the same time; this is the meeting of sky with sky.

Chapter 5, *Vajrasattva Meditation Purifying All Errors and Obscurations*, was written by C.R. Lama to complete the teachings of Chetsangpa that form Chapters 1, 3 and 5 of SIMPLY BEING[3]. He was insistent that the most important factor in Dharma practice is faith, not just faith in the meditation deities, but in ourselves, in our true nature, our buddha nature, our primordial purity. Vajrasattva, Indestructible Being, is the guarantor of our awakening. He is the presence of our presence; our purity revealed to us through the purity of a form which is emptiness itself. This brief text gives the key instructions for the practice and was written some forty years ago by Chimed Rigdzin Lama while he was living in Bengal, India.

This chapter deals with the relation between fantasy and actuality. Actuality, in this definition, is not the substantial world that seems to be revealed by our senses and understood by our thoughts. Actuality is the non-dual given, that which endures when the constructs of artifice are no longer promoted. The world of ordinary experience with its hopes and fears, its sense of good and bad, and its ceaseless conceptual organisation, is revealed as a fantasy, the product of a primary delusion.

It is exactly because our faults, errors, confusions and so on are, like everything else that occurs, devoid of inherent self-nature, that they can be quickly dissolved. The meditation of Vajrasattva, through its linking of the ordinary, the symbolic and the openness of direct presence, provides a means of dissolving our contaminated reifi-cations, creators of so much pain and guilt, into their own intrinsic purity. The essence of the practice lies in contacting and recognising the innate purity of everything that occurs. Defilement is an adven-titious phantom which thrives on the misidentification of a self. The practice provides one of the many ways into the experience of aware-ness and emptiness which is the beginning of dzogchen.

Chapters 6, *Padmasambhava Introduces Himself*, Chapter 7, *Padma-sambhava: Meaningful to Behold*, and Chapter 8, *Padmasambhava's Predictions*, concern Padmasambhava and were translated by C.R. Lama from parts of texts that were available in India in the 1960s. When the Tibetans had to leave Tibet due to Chinese control, many texts were lost. Gradually more texts have reappeared and are being reprinted but these short extracts point back to a time when every scrap was carefully treasured and preserved.

Chapters 6 and 7 address the healing power and qualities of Padma-sambhava, sustaining and curative factors that were especially impor-tant for the refugees who had lost so much. His power to do good arises not so much from worldly position as from his natural basis, the dharmadhātu, from which he summons all that is required by those who have faith in him.

Chapter 8 lists some of the many predictions made by Padma-sambhava regarding future times. Mainly they are predictions of trouble and disaster – and paradoxically these reminders of the troubles of samsara are reassuring in difficult times. We tend to over-invest our own tragedies with great importance when they are mere exemplars of the nature of dualistic experience.

Chapter 9, *Extracts from Prefaces*, offers a few extracts from prefaces which C.R. Lama dictated for a range of ritual texts published in India. They give a flavour of his phrasing and intent.

Chapter 10, *Brief Teachings*, comprises a range of short notes made when C.R. Lama was explaining texts. He talked very quickly and demanded full attention. These notes give a sense of the condensed and direct way he made his points. They have meanings which are revealed by calm reflection on one's own existence.

Chapters 11 to 16 were dictated by C.R. Lama. I wrote them down in draft form and checked the facts with Rinpoche. Some of them were then edited for presentation at conferences while others remained in note form until recently. Every effort has been made to give the correct spellings of place names but some inaccuracy may still have occurred.

Chapter 11, *Khordong Monastery*, gives an account of the history and development of C.R. Lama's main monastery in East Tibet. It describes so many people's effort in building, teaching, practising – all impermanent and all of great value. This brief description highlights the lineage transmission as the central thread binding and shaping all the monastic activity.

Chapter 12, *Education in Khordong Monastery*, is a short paper C.R. Lama gave at a conference in India. It describes the system of education at Khordong Monastery, outlining both the syllabus and the way of studying.

Chapter 13, *Khordong Monastery: Annual Cycle of Rituals*, describes the meditation practices taught and employed at Khordong Monastery. Many of them were organised according to the Jangter system of Dorje Drag Monastery. This chapter shows the annual cycle of meditation rituals. It was presented at a conference in Varanasi, India, along with Chapter 12.

Chapter 14, *New Year Celebrations*, gives an account of the New Year celebrations in Kham Trehor district, as celebrated by monks and lay people.

Chapter 15, *Comments on Culture*, offers C.R. Lama's reflections on local culture and gives a glimpse of the way of life within which his sense of the world was developed. Rinpoche was unsentimental and accepted with equanimity the many changing circumstances of his life and the irrevocable loss of traditional Tibetan culture.

Chapter 16, **Rigdzin Godem and Sikkim,** gives a brief account of Rigdzin Godem revealing the hidden land of Sikkim. It includes a short prayer. Rinpoche presented this paper at a conference in Sikkim in 1979 and it is an example of the way he would subvert the objectifying academic structure by turning the focus towards practice.

C.R. Lama also wrote a Butterlamp Prayer to sustain his Guru's health and long life. It has already been printed separately as RADIANT ASPIRATION [4], and so is not included here.

The dharma itself never changes but the forms of its true expression are myriad, arising due to the karmic texture of different times. C.R. Lama was an unrepeatable presence – just as we all are when we free ourselves from the constrictions of assumptions and habits. Being, presence, is always fresh, always open, always ready to spontaneously show what is useful and fitting. This was ground, path and result radiantly present as C.R. Lama.

> *Light radiates ceaselessly from the enlightened mind:*
> *may it shine from Rinpoche's heart wherever he resides*
> *Turning all beings towards their own true nature.*

James Low

NOTES

[1] Low, J. *BEING GURU RINPOCHE: A COMMENTARY ON NUDEN DORJE'S TERMA, VIDYADHARA GURU SADHANA,* (Trafford, 2006).

[2] Dudjom Rinpoche, Jikdrel Yeshe Dorje. Dorje, G. (Tr and Ed). *THE NYINGMA SCHOOL OF TIBETAN BUDDHISM: ITS FUNDAMENTALS AND HISTORY,* (Wisdom Publications, Boston, 1991).

[3] Low J. *SIMPLY BEING: TEXTS IN THE DZOGCHEN TRADITION,* 3rd ed., (CPI Antony Rowe, November 2010).

[4] Lama, C.R. and Low, J. *RADIANT ASPIRATION: THE BUTTERLAMP PRAYER LAMP OF ASPIRATION,* (Simply Being, July 2011).

1

Vajrayāna in Tibet

Here is a brief account of vajrayāna tantric[1] practice in Tibet according to the Nyingma School.

According to the *Mani bKa 'Bum*, the collection of teachings on the mantra of Avalokiteśvara, King Songtsen Gampo (*Srong-bTsan sGam-Po*) spoke about the various tantric views and meditations. He had much to say about the developing stage (*utpannakrama*), the completion stage (*sampannakrama*) and instructions (*upadeśa*) of the practice of Ārya Avalokiteśvara. The whole of Tibet became devoted to Ārya Avalokiteśvara, Chenresi, and started meditating on the six syllables (*Om Mani Padme Hūm*) from the time of this king [7th century a.d.]. Some tantric texts were translated when the Indians Ācārya Kusara and Brahmāna Śaṅkara and the Nepalese Ācārya Śīlamañju went to Tibet. Some small portion of the tantras of Ārya Avalokiteśvara were translated. After five generations, King Trisong Detsen (*Khri Srong lDeu bTsan*) invited the great scholar Śāntarakṣita and the great sage Mahācārya Padmasambhava and other Indian scholars, who then came to Tibet and propagated Buddhism there. Mahācārya Dharmakīrti, the great scholar Vimalamitra, Ācārya Buddhaguhya and Ācārya Śāntigarbha all went to Tibet. Mahācārya Dharmakīrti transmitted the method of consecration in the Yoga Tantra Vajradhātu Maṇḍala. Mahāpaṇḍita Vimalamitra and others taught the Tibetan people whatever was necessary. Tibetan translators Vairocana, Ma (*rMa*), Nyag (*gNyag*) and Nub (*gNub*) etc. translated a large number of texts including the Kᴜɴ Bʏᴇᴅ ʀGʏᴀʟ Pᴏ, Tʜᴇ Aʟʟ-Aᴄᴄᴏᴍᴘʟɪꜱʜɪɴɢ Kɪɴɢ, the ᴍDᴏ ᴅGᴏɴɢꜱ 'Dᴜꜱ, Tʜᴇ Sᴜᴛʀᴀ ᴛʜᴀᴛ Uɴɪꜰɪᴇꜱ ᴛʜᴇ Iɴᴛᴇɴᴛɪᴏɴꜱ, one of the four root tantras of Anuyoga, and the ꜱGʏᴜ 'Pʜʀᴜʟ 'Gʀᴜʙ ꜱDᴇ ʙʀGʏᴀᴅ, Tʜᴇ Eɪɢʜᴛ Sᴇᴄᴛɪᴏɴꜱ ᴏꜰ Pʀᴀᴄᴛɪᴄᴇ ᴏꜰ Iʟʟᴜꜱᴏʀʏ Fᴏʀᴍꜱ, and so on. The basic texts (*āgamas*) and explanations (*upadeśas*) were also translated.

Mahācārya Padmasambhava through his miraculous power brought to Tibet many tantric works from India, Uḍḍiyāna and so on and translated them. Other tantras which were prevalent in India went to Tibet in the course of time.

The Emergence of Tantra

Twenty-eight years after his nirvāṇa, Lord Buddha incarnated himself in the form of Guhyapati, the Master of Secrets, at Mount Malaya in South India. There he found five wise beings, known as 'The Five Excellent Ones of Sublime Nobility', who could expound three external tantras and eighteen internal tantras. These five wise beings belonged to the five groups of sentient beings:

1. From the pure family of the gods, devasatkūla, came Yaśasvī Varapāla (*Grags-lDan mChog-mKyongs*)
2. From the pure family of the yakṣas, yakṣasatkūla, came Ulkāmukha (*sKar-mDa' gDong*)
3. From the pure family of the nagas, nāgasatkūla, came King Takṣaka (*kLu-rGyal 'Jog-Po*)
4. From the pure family of the rākṣasa, rākṣasasatkūla, came Matyaupāyika (*bLo-Gros Thabs-lDan*)
5. From the pure family of the humans, manuṣasatkūla, came Vimalakīrti (*Li-Tsa-Bi Dri-Med Grags-Pa*)

Of these five wise beings, it was the rākṣasa, Lodrö Thabden (*bLo-Gros Thabs-lDan*) who wrote the tantras on golden leaves with azure beryl ink and kept them concealed in the sky according to the seven instructions of Guhyapati. These seven instructions are as follows:

1. The tantra was to be written on gold leaf
2. The ink used must be of beryl stone
3. The tantra should be kept in a container made of precious stones

4. The container must be kept in a place which is free of destruction by the elements

5. Devīs, goddesses, were placed to guard the container

6. King Ja was placed in charge of the tantras

7. Kukurāja, Uparāja and other teachers were predicted, even up to the present day

When the time was ripe, King Ja [or Dza] had a dream in which he saw that the tantras written on gold leaf were being bestowed on him. This dream came true by the morning when all the tantras rained down on the roof of his house. After this King Ja, Buddhaguhya, Buddhajñāna, Ānandavajra and others expounded these tantras to the world.

These eighteen tantras and the *MAHĀMĀYA GUHYASĀRA, SECRET ESSENCE OF GREAT ILLUSION*, were thoroughly studied by Buddhaguhya, Mahāpaṇḍita Vimalamitra and the Translators Ma and Nyag. Mahācārya Mahāhuṅkāra taught his disciples, such as Namkhai Nyingpo (*Nam-mKha'i sNying-Po*) of Nub, the Viśuddha sādhana and other tantras. Padmasambhava taught other disciples the Kilaya sādhana and the Mahāṣṭa sādhana. Buddhajñāna, a Tibetan, and Vyākaraṇavajra and others taught the people. Thus have their teachings come down to the present day.

Regarding the āgama anuyoga, the samājasūtra, the vidyasūtra and so on, the instructions were given by four Indian and Nepali ācāryas to the Tibetan, Buddhajñāna, whose work has come down to the present day. The cycle of texts *bSHAD rGYUD DGONGS PA 'DUS PA, EXPLANATORY TANTRA ASSEMBLY OF CLARITY, (SAMKṢIPTA SANDHISAMGRAHA)* was translated at Samye Monastery in Central Tibet during the early translation period.

Mahāsampanna atiyoga is divided into three sections:

The eighteen external instructions of the Mind Section, (*cittavarga, Sems-sDe*) were expounded. These instructions were expounded by Vairocana and Yudra Nyingpo (*gYu-sGra-sNying-Po*) and have been transmitted to the present day.

The Internal Space Section (*dhātuvarga, kLong sDe*) instructions were presented by Śrī Siṅgha and expounded by Vairocana and have been transmitted to the present day.

The essential instructions contained in the seventeen Secret Oral Section (*upadeśavarga, Man-Ngag-sDe*) tantras were expounded by Ācārya Padmasambhava, Vimalamitra and Vairocana and have been transmitted to the present day.

A Short Account of the Meaning of Vajrayāna

The sNGA-'GYUR KUN-BYED-RGYAL-PO, EARLY TRANSLATION ALL-ACCOMPLISHING KING, states, "*Theg-Pa rNam-Pa gNyis-Yin-Te mTshan-Nyid rGyu-Yi-Theg-Pa 'Bras-Bu sNgags-Kyi-Theg-Pa.*" That is, "*There are two kinds of yana or vehicle. The first is the vehicle which functions as a cause and relies on signs and analysis. The second is the vehicle which functions according to the result and relies on tantra.*" Yana indicates lifting, raising up to enlightenment. The vehicle of the cause (*lakṣaṇa hetuyāna*) is set forth in the sutras. The vehicle of the result (*phala vajrayāna*) refers to mantrayāna, tantrayāna and sahajayāna. Because of its power and efficacy, phala vajrayāna is considered to be superior to lakṣaṇa hetuyāna, the path that functions as a cause for the gaining of enlightenment at a later date. There are many followers of the vajrayāna who have attained liberation, often with their body being transformed into a rainbow.

The path of tantra is called the 'vajrayana', the diamond or indestructible path. The diamond is said to have seven qualities:

1. A diamond cannot be cut by anything
2. A diamond cannot be destroyed
3. A diamond is a real stone
4. A diamond is very strong
5. A diamond maintains its shape
6. A diamond is impenetrable
7. A diamond can penetrate anything

Buddhists believe that tantra has all these seven virtues which each manifest many qualities. Of these, only one quality is given here for each of the virtues listed above. The vajrayana demonstrates the indestructible buddha nature, Vajradhara, in all beings. It holds that Vajradhara:

1. Is immune from all contamination

2. Cannot be destroyed
3. Is the real nirvāṇa
4. Is strength
5. Is firmness
6. Is immortal
7. Is the only means of the liberation of the world

Three Vehicles

The teachings have been organised according to various schemas. One found in the early translations of the Nyingma tradition employs three vehicles or paths:

1. The path of the vehicle that leads out of suffering, sarvobhava-nayaka yāna (*Kun-Byung-'Dren*)
2. The path of the vehicle that groups around austerity, tapasvinkūla yāna (*dKa'-Thub Rigs-Pa*)
3. The path of the vehicle of the methods which overpower, śaktiupāya yāna (*dBang-bsGyur Thabs-Kyi Theg-Pa*)

These are the names given in the Old Translations [Nyingma].

Nine Vehicles

The more generally used schema employes nine vehicles:

1. The vehicle of the listeners, śrāvakayāna (*sNyan-Thos-Kyi Theg-Pa*)
2. The vehicle of the solitary buddhas, pratyekabuddhayāna (*Rang-rGyal-Kyi Theg-Pa*)
3. The vehicle of the altruistic bodhisattvas, bodhisattvayāna (*Byang-Chub Sems-Pa'i Theg-Pa*)

These above three constitute the sarvabhavanayakayāna

4. The vehicle of activity, kriyāyāna (*Bya-rGyud*)
5. The vehicle of conduct, caryāyāna (*sPyod-rGyud*)
6. The vehicle which is supreme, anuttarayāna (*bLa-Na-Med-Pa'i rGyud*), also known as the vehicle of yoga meditation, Yogayāna (*rNal-'Byor rGyud*)

These above three constitute the tapasvinkūlayāna

7. The vehicle of the father tantras, pitrāgayāna (Pha-rGyud), also known as mahāyoga

8. The vehicle of the mother tantras matṛyagayāna (*Ma-rGyud*), also known as āgama anuyoga

9. The vehicle of the non-dual yoga, advayayogayāna (*atiyogayāna*) (*gNyis-Med-rGyud*), also known as mahāsampanna atiyoga Advayayogayāna itself has three sections:

a. The mind section, cittavarga (*Sems-dDe*)

b. The space section, khavarga (*kLong-sDe*)

c. The secret oral section, upadeśavarga (*Man-Ngag-sDe*)

These above three constitute the śaktiupāyayāna

The first three vehicles belong to the sutra system of the vehicle of cause, relying on signs. The remaining six belong to the vehicle of the result, employing vajrayāna teaching to gain knowledge and power. The *tapasvinkūlayāna*, comprising of the first three tantric paths, is restrictive in its focus whereas the second three are more open in their view.

According to mahāyoga there is no hard-and-fast rule for determining what is virtuous and what is unvirtuous since everything is naturally pure from the very beginning and unchangeable. It is human knowledge which sees differences and makes judgements. Awakening to our natural situation is the only means to obtain enlightenment (*abhisambodh*).

According to āgama anuyoga, awareness (*vidyā*) is naturally full of clarity and bliss (*mahānanda*).

According to the mahāsampanna atiyoga, there is no need to refer to the past or to the future, nor to look to cause and effect. In the present moment, awareness (*vidyā*) is itself inherent in the three bodies or modes of enlightenment, dharmakāya, sambhogakāya and nirmāṇakāya.

The dharmakāya (*Chos-sKu*) or mode of actuality is formless and without substance yet is the source of all enlightenment. It is the absolute truth of saṃsāra, being self-existing and everlasting. It is represented by Samantabhadra or Ādi-Buddha.

The sambhogakāya (*kLong-sKu*) or mode of enjoyment is glorious and beautiful. It is both the natural effulgence of the dharmakāya and the reward or fulfilment of the Buddha's merit. It is represented by the Buddhas of the five families, who are graceful and blissful.

The nirmāṇakāya (sPrul-sKu) or mode of participation is the Buddhas' enlightening presence, leading sentient beings from darkness to light, from sleep to awakening, from ignorance to presence. It is represented by Buddha Śākyamuni who showed the emptiness and lack of inherent self-nature in all phenomena.

Mahāsampanna atiyoga is divided into three sections: cittavarga, khavarga and upadeśavarga.

According to the mind series (cittavarga, Sems-dDe) whatever you see, feel, touch and so on is nothing other than reflections of your mind (citta). This knowledge is naturally present for the mind itself is awareness, clarity and emptiness – pure and without defilement. Therefore the mind does not require anything external for its purification. In the mind series the focus is on the subject (dharmatā) whereas in mahāmudrā the focus is on the object (dharma).

According to the space series (khavarga, or dhātuvarga, kLong-sDe) the view is that all phenomena (dharmas) are contained in the actuality of awareness (dharmatā, Samantabhadra) hence it rejects the introduction of interpretations presented by human knowledge. This view does not need any sin or object to be removed, purified or transformed. It itself is the depth and light of intrinsic knowing or awareness. With the practice of the indestructible mode (vajrakāya sādhana) the body of the meditator (sādhaka) manifests as a rainbow. There are many followers of this practice whose rainbow-like body has melted into the jñānakāya, the mode of integration of the three modes of enlightenment. They include Vimalamitra, Jñānasūtra, Jñānagarbha between the ninth and eleventh centuries, and Pema Dudul (Padma dDud-'Dul) and Tsangkor Drubchen (rTshang-sKor Grub-Chen) in the twentieth century.

Dhātuvarga highlights the non-duality of openness or depth (śūnyatā) and light. This can appear similar to the Rim lNga (panchkram) view held in the Gelugpa tradition. However that view states that the five winds (pañcavāyu) in the body are to be controlled and thus śūnyatā is to be achieved gradually. It means that in order to achieve śūnyatā and light one has to strive, whereas in dhātuvarga there is no such striving to achieve light.

According to the secret oral series (*upadeśavarga, Man-Ngag-sDe*) the view is concerned with awakening to the nature of one's existence. Non-dual clarity (*advayajñāna*) is free of both gain or loss for it sees and shows the emptiness (*śūnyatā*) of the object (*dharma*) and of the subject (*dharmatā*), and of saṃsāra and nirvāṇa. Therefore there is no stress on sādhana. By the light of this awareness (*jñānavidyā*) dharmatā gains self-knowledge easily. Then all kinds of reasoning cease and nothing remains to be done.

Upadeśavarga focuses on the experience of a direct object and so it can look like the six unions (*ṣaḍaṅga-yoga, sByor-Drug*) practised in the Gelugpa tradition but these two are different. sByor-Drug shuts the five winds in the central channel (*avadhūti*) and tries to remain in emptiness in order to gain supreme happiness (*mahānanda*) whereas upadeśavarga leaves aside all the thoughts in the mind and rests in intrinsic awareness, our natural presence.

Upadeśavarga doctrine reveals the enlightened mode of primordial awareness (*jñānakāya*) which will take form like a rainbow and, in that, it is considered superior to the dhātuvarga doctrine. In dhātuvarga there are only three doors, body, voice and mind (*kāya, vāk* and *citta*) whereas in the view of upadeśavarga, the advayatattva or dharmatā samapta dṛṣṭi, all the three doors are merged in jñānakāya.

These three series, cittavarga (*Sems-sDe*), dhātuvarga (*kLongs-Sde*), and upadeśavarga (*Man-Ngag-sDe*), together constitute the view and practice that is known as the great completion (*mahāsampanna, rDzogs-Chen*), and there is a reason for this name. All dharmas which are possible in the realms of becoming (*bhavadṛṣṭi, saṃsāra*) and in nirvāṇa are contained in emptiness (*śūnyatā*) and intrinsic awareness (*vidyājñāna*) and that is why it is complete (*sampannatā*). Pure (*śuddha*) and impure (*aśuddha*) thoughts which occur with the clarity and emptiness of awareness (*vidyāprākaśaśūnyatā*) are called all-pervading compassion (*karuṇāsarvavibhu*). They are also called the view of non-dual emptiness (*dṛṣṭiśūnyatā advaya*). There is no other way to liberation (*mukti*) except the above-mentioned three series, hence they are called great (*mahā*).

The self (*atma*) is the self-luminosity of awareness. It originates from emptiness (*śūnyatā*). It is completely pure (*viśuddha*). That is why awareness (*vidyā*) and emptiness (*śūnyatā*) are called non-dual (*advaya*). Emptiness is self-arising self-perfecting (*svayamvibhusiddhi*). Emptiness and radiance (*prakāśa*) are non-dual (*advaya*).

Due to ignorance (*avidyā*), different kinds of thought arise and this is what is called the mind (*citta*). Due to the absence of ignorance, the object (*grāhya*) and the subject (*grāhaka*) are free of conceptual elaboration (*prapañcarahita*) and are clarity and emptiness alone (*prakāśunyatarahita*).

Awareness inseparable from intrinsic knowing (*vidyājñāna*) is both the source and the site of the integration of awareness and mental activity. Whatever is perceived is within the mind (*citta*) and the mind is emptiness (*śūnyatā*). Emptiness is non-duality, the union of experience and emptiness. By comprehending this all-encompassing awareness-emptiness, all phenomena (*dharma*) become clear. This is the way of awakening to the presence of awareness (*vidyā*).

Objects germinate within the mind (*citta*) which is emptiness (*śūnyatā*), which is unchanging presence and light. When one understands this, which is everything, one abides in knowing the great completion (*mahāsampannatā*).

According to this view it is not necessary to follow structured meditation for the teaching of a guru is sufficient to obtain wisdom. If one fails to obtain wisdom from the teachings of a guru, even then one will gain it in the bardo.

Wisdom is purity itself. It is therefore necessary for us to abide in it as it is and not contaminate it by unnecessary reliance on our thoughts. For example, the sun is always bright yet it can be hidden by the clouds and vapours created by its own heat. Similarly there are elements that obscure wisdom but they are inseparable from wisdom and so we must abide in wisdom at all times and in all situations.

This is made clear in the following extract from Chapter 4 of THE PRAYER IN SEVEN CHAPTERS (GSOL 'DEBS LE'U BDUN MA)[2] by Padmasambhava.

> *"As regards the eye's objects which are the appearances of absolutely all the outer and inner entities which constitute the universe and its inhabitants, maintain the openness of allowing these appearances to arise yet without grasping at them as being*

something inherently real. See that they are the radiant forms of clarity and emptiness, pure and naturally free from graspable objects and grasping mind.

As regards the ear's objects of the sounds which are held to as being pleasant or unpleasant, for all sounds maintain the openness of sound and emptiness free of all involved discriminating thought. This is sound and emptiness, the unborn and unobstructed Buddhas' speech.

As regards the objects of our mentation, the restless movement of the five afflicting poisons'[3] thoughts, do not enter upon the intellect's artificial activities of awaiting future thoughts and following after past thoughts. By leaving the restless movement as it is, we are liberated in the Dharmakaya.

Outwardly, see that all the appearances of graspable objects are pure. Inwardly, experience the liberation of your grasping mind. With this non-duality of outer and inner, experience the clarity of seeing your own nature."

The entire view rests on three points:

1. Not to rely on the outer objects which constitute this world
2. To keep the mind uninvolved in the inner thoughts which arise
3. By observing these two points, light or clarity, and depth or emptiness, are revealed as the actuality of one's own nature.

The great completion (*mahāsampanna*) has three aspects: source (*mūla*), path (*mārga*) and result (*phala*). The source, or root, or ground (*mūla*) is awareness (*vidyā*), that has from the very beginning been free of and untouched by all the diverse thoughts, good and bad, which constitute saṃsāra and nirvāṇa. It is not soiled by worldly delusions. This natural purity, which is intrinsically free in the past, present and future, is the source.

The path or way (*mārga*) is awareness (*vidyā*) which is free from good and evil and also from the absence of good and evil. It is emptiness (*śunyata*) and is like the centre of the clear blue sky. This is called the path.

The result (*phala*) is awareness (*vidyā*), which fulfills all the requirements of the path and without effort attains the natural purity, depth and light.

There are Two Styles of Practice for Source, Path and Result:

1. The vast and profound primordial purity of 'cutting through' (*Yang-Zab Ka-Dag Khregs-Chod*) also described as 'indirect experience'.
2. The infinite immediacy of 'direct spontaneity' (*rGya-Che-Ba Lhun-Grub Thod-rGal*) also described as 'direct experience'.

Cutting Through, or Indirect Experience

Wisdom or natural awareness has not made any error by which new things were created. Therefore there was no need of a Buddha, because wisdom is purity itself. Thus knowledge itself is always already within wisdom and is known by the name of Dharmakāya Samantabhadra or Mahāmāta Prajñāpāramitā Dharmakāya. The absence of wisdom brings ignorance, desire and anger which are the roots of all afflictions. Afflictions have six main forms: ignorance, mental dullness, desire, anger, pride and jealousy. They cast us into the net of the twelve links in the chain of interdependent co-origination (*pratītyasamutpāda*). These are as follows:

1. avidyā, ignorance
2. saṃskāra, associations and assumptions
3. vijñāna, consciousness
4. nāma-rūpa, name and form
5. satāyatana, the six sense organs
6. sparśa, contact
7. vedanā, feelings
8. tṛṣṇā, craving or hankering after
9. upadāna, sensual enthrallment
10. bhava, procreation
11. jāti, birth
12. jara-maraṇa, old age and death

Due to error and sin (*pāpa*) which fetter us and pull us down, a person has to pass through the six realms of existence, namely: hell (*naraka*); hungry ghost (*preta*); animal (*tiryagyoni*); human (*manuṣya*); demi-god (*asūra*); and god (*sūra* or *deva*).

All the linked stages from ignorance to death arise due to ignorance of wisdom. They are illusions devoid of inherent self nature. Wisdom is untouched by saṃsāra or nirvāṇa. It is depth and light and bright like the sun, full of empathy, kindness and clarity. Thought arising from knowledge within the six realms cannot affect wisdom which has natural depth, light and empathic responsivity. Having no form of any kind, wisdom is unbiased and all-pervading, like oil in a sesame seed. Natural wisdom is concealed by reification and attachment embedded in the ignorance-pervaded ground consciousness (*ālayavijñanā avidyā*). Therefore one should not act according to the thoughts arising from human knowledge.

It should always be borne in mind that natural wisdom is everywhere, especially when temptation comes down forcefully like water from the top of a mountain. Do not think of the subject or object, but remain neutral, then you will know and attain wisdom, as the three inseparable modes of enlightenment (*dharmakāya, sambhogakāya* and *nirmāṇakāya*). Even sacred deeds, theoretical or practical, need not be performed as these are also contained within wisdom. There is no need for investigating activity or its result. By gaining wisdom, happiness (*ānanda*) and light (*jyoti*), will increase. With this one will not pay any heed to thoughts that spring up from human knowledge. This is the final destination of all and everything.

Direct Spontaneity or Direct Experience

According to the view of direct spontaneity set out in THE TREASURY OF PRECIOUS PEARLS, MU-TIG RIN-PO-CHE PHRENG-BA:

> Lus-Kyi-gNad-Ni-rNam-gSum-sTe Seng-Ge'i-Tshul Dang gLang-Chen-Tshul Drang-Srong-lTa-Bur-Zhes-Par-Bya.
>
> *"Thus one should adopt the meditation postures of the three modes of enlightenment. For dharmakāya one should stand or sleep like a lion. For sambhogakāya one should stand or sleep like an elephant. For nirmāṇakāya one should sit like a rishi or sage."*

In practising thus, one has to remain silent. One's teeth should not be closed together in one's mouth. Breathe gently. By breathing out one's internal uneasiness will be expelled. Thus the mind remains firm in its wisdom. Body and mind should be kept as before.

Depth (*śūnyatā*), light (*jyoti*) and empathic participation (*Thugs rJe*) have six lamps which let one see four objects.

Six Lamps, sGron-Ma Drug

1. Tsit-Ta Sha-Yi sGron-Ma

   This lamp represents the heart from which four golden qualities arise: wisdom, depth, light and naturalness, or empathic participation. The core of the heart is Buddha. Wisdom, depth, light and naturalness or empathic participation are centred therein.

2. rTsa-Dar dKar-Lam-Gyi sGron-Ma

   The channels are like white silk. Of these channels, two have come out like the horns of a snail and extend to the retinas. These channels are clear and pure and this lamp is called 'the way of the white channel', through which flow depth, light, wisdom and empathy.

3. rGyang-Zhag Chu'i sGron-Ma

   It is the connecting channel between the eye and the heart whereby wisdom gives sight. All things are thus seen and called Samantabhadra.

4. dByings rNam-Dag-Gi sGron-Ma

   If you concentrate and gaze at the blue sky, the colour lightens and becomes clear through wisdom, and that is called 'pure natural light'.

5. Thig-Le sTong-Pa'i sGron-Ma

   It is the vision of the sphere of emptiness. One sees rays of different colours and therein you find many small particles which are all empty spheres.

6. Rig-Pa rDo-rJe Lug-Gu-rGyud Shes-Rab Rang-Byung-Gi sGron-Ma

   This lamp is the self-existing wisdom light (*jñānapradīpa*). It is like the blue sky (*dhātu*), an empty sphere (*bindu*), and the colour of a peacock's tail. From it rain appears, falling like knotted hair or strings of pearls, or garlands of flowers. In them is seen wisdom like the blue sky where the empty sphere (*binduśūnyatā*) is seen and wherein we find the supreme wisdom (*parāvidyā*) that does not disappear. The blue sky is the sign of the source (*mūla*); the empty sphere (*bīndu, Thig-Le*) is the sign of the path; and with the wisdom of total quiescence (*sarvashestajñāna*), the supreme wisdom (*parāvidyā*), there are rays of light, the sign of empathy, the result.

Wisdom and the Three Modes of Enlightenment (*Triparākāya, sKu-gSum*)

Wisdom is not created by thought or brain or prepared by anything. It is primordial, self-originated and there is no reason for its being. It is purity itself from the very beginning and is the actual truth. It is reliable, unchanging and undeceptive.   Its characteristic is depth (*śūnyatā*). These are the characteristics of the natural mode (*dharmakāya*).

This wisdom cannot be destroyed by the four elements. Due to its brightness that gives light to all, it cannot be covered or concealed by the five afflictions (*kleśas*) of anger, desire, stupidity, jealousy and pride, nor by the three main afflictions of anger, desire and stupidity. All the above are the characteristics of the mode of enjoyment (*sambhogakāya*).

After obtaining wisdom, one should be satisfied with it, for there is no delusion in it. For the good of saṃsāra at any moment wisdom can cause compassionate illusory manifestation. These are the characteristics of the mode of participation (*nirmaṇakāya*).

Five Paths, Mārgas, in relation to Wisdom

1. The path of accumulation (*sambhāramārga, Tshogs-Lam*) is the way to attain wisdom. Sambhāramārga means to gather the accumulation of merit in order to attain wisdom.
2. The path of joining (*prayogamārga, sByor-Lam*) is to practise, to be active in attaining wisdom.
3. The path of seeing (*darśanamārga, mThong-Lam*) means that after completion of the first two paths, one sees or knows wisdom.
4. The path of contemplation (*bhāvanāmārga, sGom-Lam*) occurs when wisdom is seen or known. Then there is no ground for uncertainty or doubt, and so all uncertainties disappear.
5. The path of no more learning (*aśaikṣamārga, Mi-sLob-Lam*) or the supreme path (*anuttaramārga*) is entered by completing the previous four paths and so one abides in wisdom.

Ten Stages of Wisdom

These stages have no connection with the first two of the five paths listed above. Stages one to seven are connected with the third path, the path of seeing. Stages eight and nine are connected with the fourth path, the path of contemplation. Stage ten is connected with the fifth path, the path of no more learning.

1. The stage of supreme happiness (*pramuditābhūmi*). With the path of seeing, darśanamārga, the truth of actuality, dharmatā-satya, wisdom is seen or known and all thoughts are insepa-rable from emptiness, bringing great happiness.

2. The stage of purity (*vimalābhūmi*). In seeing or knowing wisdom it becomes clear that wisdom is the source and is free from all limitation.

3. The stage of light (*prabhākarībhūmi*). In seeing or knowing wisdom there is light and clarity. This means that all actions are complete.

4. The stage of light manifesting (*arciṣmatībhūmi*). In seeing or knowing wisdom, there is the knowledge that depth, light and so on are inseparable in non-duality.

5. The stage of the unavoidable (*sudurjayābhūmi*). In seeing or knowing wisdom, even the smallest thought of suffering, or of subject, or of object, vanishes.

6. The stage of confronting (*abhimukhībhūmi*). With wisdom, its power makes clear all learning and divine modes.

7. The stage of release from contamination (*duraṁgamābhūmi*). After obtaining wisdom, all thoughts derived from human knowledge clear away.

The seven bhūmis [stages] listed above are called 'the unclean seven bhūmis' (aśuddhasaptabhūmi).

8. The stage of the unchangeable (*acalābhūmi*). The self-existing sphere of awareness (*vidyājñānabindusvabhāva*) is the accom-plishment of all-pervading non-duality (*advayavibhusiddhi*) and is therefore called 'the unchangeable stage'.

9. The stage of good intellect (*sādhumatībhūmi*). By gaining wisdom, one becomes the self-existing light (*swayaṁprakāśa*).

10. The stage of the holy cloud (*dharmameghābhūmi*). Space (*dhātu*), wisdom (*vidyā*) and awareness (*jñāna*) are inherently pure and clear, being inseparable from emptiness.

These three stages listed above are called the 'three pure and clear stages' (viśuddhatribhūmi).

Six Further Stages Specific to the Vajrayāna

1. The stage of the source of all (*sarvaprabhava bhūmi*). This means that light and power (*śakti*) are always available. One who attains this stage fully attains the vibhusiddhibhūmi.

2. The stage of freedom from worldly desires (*akāmāpadmavana bhūmi*). This stage is free of desire and avarice and so cannot be touched by any harm.

3. The stage which is indestructible (*vajradhara bhūmi*). With this stage nothing can destroy one's clarity, so it is like the vajra.

4. The stage of the wisdom of great bliss of all experience (*jñānacakramahāsambara bhūmi*). When one gains this stage one can see the divine maṇḍala and can also make others see it.

5. The stage of undisturbed absorption (*mahāsamādhi bhūmi*). After attaining this stage one lives in wisdom and nothing can separate one from it.

6. The stage of wisdom mastery (*jñānaguru bhūmi*). After gaining this stage, wisdom becomes self-arising so it is called 'the stage of effortless mastery'.

The above six stages belong to the stage of universal benefit (sarvaprabhāva bhūmi).

With the attainment of this stage, one has completed all the stages of wisdom and so becomes a master of the great perfection, mahāsampanna, and is endowed with power to do good in the world.

The Four Visions, or Visionary Experiences, their Jurisdictions and Results, showing the Six Lamps

1. The vision of the revelation of actuality (*dharmatā abhimuktidṛṣṭi, Chos-Nyid mNgon-Sum-Gyi sNang-Ba*): actuality becomes clear with the dropping of interpretation. Rays in the sky come out of the sun, likewise everything comes out of wisdom. Empty

spheres (*śūnyatābīndu, Thig Le*) and light are visible from the chakra at the nose-ridge between the eyebrows (*ajñācakra*). With the revelation of actuality, thought creation in the mind disappears and thus one manifests all the qualities of the Buddhas.

2. The vision of ever-increasing meditative experiences (*rNyams Gong-'Phel-Gyi sNang-Ba*): the experiences of practice develop. When one gets direct wisdom there is contentment, impartiality, strength and freedom from illusion. Visions like a rainbow become visible, increase and become clear. One is liberated between death and rebirth.

3. The vision of awareness free of limit (*Rig-Pa Tshad-Phebs-Kyi sNang-Ba*): correct understanding coming like the rising sun. Wisdom has no birth but is self-existing. From the beginning it is purity, truth and righteousness. It experiences no binding of any kind. It is bright. It has no birth or stoppage and no illusion of any kind. All the bodies of human beings will merge into it like a rainbow.

   Regarding the jurisdiction:
   External Jurisdiction. At this time one will forget all things but will see the divine realms (*devakṣetra*).
   Internal Jurisdiction. One who has gained wisdom will become pure and reach the level of deities and the supreme light and will be confirmed with supreme light (*mahāsandhi abhiṣeka*).
   Central Jurisdiction. Mind becomes pure and sees emptiness (*śūnyatā*) face to face without any obscurations or afflictions (*kleśa*).

   Regarding the result:
   Through this vision, one is liberated in the mode of enjoyment (*sambhogakāya*).

4. The vision of the fulfilment of actuality itself (*dharmatā-samāptadṛṣti, Chos-Nyid Zad-Pa'i sNang-Ba*): all limitations and obstacles end in the self-dissolving actuality (*dharmatā*). With this there is an end to external objects, and internal thoughts, habits and afflictions all end. At source, the power of generating such experiences also ends. Direct wisdom which is visible also ends. When this happens one merges into the jewel of self-occurring completion (*svāyamsiddhiratna*). That stage has four qualities:

i. One's knowledge fills the sky
ii. The elements have no effect, for one has become immortal.
iii. One's wisdom abides in the inseparability of enlightenment and space (*dhātubuddha*).
iv. One abides in one's rightful position which is unchanging. With this stage all obscurations to and by knowledge (*jñeyāvaraṇa*) are purified and one functions throughout all-encompassing space(*dharmadhātu*) for the good of all.

Wisdom is everywhere in saṃsāra, but when one dies without awakening the four visions this will not be recognised.

Four Powers arise due to these Four Visions

1. When one gains external jurisdiction, one will see only the divine realms.
2. When one gains internal jurisdiction, one's body is filled with rainbows and spheres (*bīndu*).
3. When one gains central jurisdiction, one has clairvoyance.
4. With the result, one overcomes birth and death and can do whatever one wishes.

This Manifests as Four Courages

1. One is not afraid of suffering.
2. Suffering and happiness are equal (*sukhaduḥkhasamatā*).
3. One is not proud of being a Buddha.
4. One does not care even if one does not gain enlightenment.

Wisdom does not arise or cease. It does not need to labour for anything. It always acts for the good of the universe.

NOTES

[1] Tantra is the view and practice which reveals the non-dual integration and continuity of all experience. It dissolves the delusion of perceiving separate real entities.

[2] Lama, C.R. and Low, J. THE SEVEN CHAPTERS OF PRAYER, AS TAUGHT BY PADMA-SAMBHAVA OF URGYEN, KNOWN IN TIBETAN AS LE'U BDUN MA, (edition khordong, 2008)

[3] Anger, desire, stupidity, pride, jealousy.

2

The Nyingma Tradition

For ordinary, small-minded people to gain the happiness of the upper realms of men and gods they must practise contemplation of the four attitude-changing thoughts (*bLo-lDog rNam-Pa bZhi*)[1], and take refuge in the Three Jewels of Buddha, Dharma and Sangha.

The Hinayana

With the Hinayana *(Theg-dMan)* paths of the Listeners, *(Śrāvaka, Nyan-Thos)* and of the Autonomous Enlightened *(Pratyekabuddha, Rang-rGyal)*, beings of medium capacity develop an attitude of revulsion for samsara and on the basis of this they attain the stages of Śrāvaka or Defeater of Limitation *(Arhat)*, or Pratyekabuddha Arhat. In order achieve this they follow the path of the Four Noble Truths *('Phags-Pa'i bDen-Pa bZhi)*[2] and the path of the three supreme trainings *(Lhag-Pa'i bsLab-Pa gSum)*[3] and thus they gain the stage of the saintly arhats *('Phags dGra-bCom-Pa)*.

The Mahayana

1. Sutra

By means of the sutra path, the general characteristics *(mTshan-Nyid)* of all phenomena *(Chos Thams-Cad)* and one's own characteristics are understood. On the basis of this, by using the six paramitas[4] and the four factors of co-operation (bsDu-Ba'i-dNgos-Po bZhi)[5] and the other aspects of the Bodhisattva's conduct and view and meditation, after a long time at the end of many numberless aeons (kalpas) one will gain the stage of Buddhahood (Byang-Chub). The method to achieve this is to perfectly develop an altruistic aspiration for enlightenment.

2. Tantra

By means of the tantric path that is for great beings, one does not examine the general characteristics of all phenomena or one's own characteristics but rather one understands the true nature of one's inner original situation (Don-Dam, absolute) and thus one gains the Buddhahood ('Tshang-rGya-Ba) of one's own true nature.

Sutra and Tantra

THE ALL ACCOMPLISHING KING (SARVAKRUTA RAJASUTRA, KUN-BYED RGYAL-PO) belonging to the earlier translation period (sNga-'Gyur, that is to say rNying-Ma) says, "There are two vehicles (Theg-Pa), the causal vehicle relying on external characteristics (sutralakshanahetuyana, mTshan-Nyid rGyu-Yi Theg-pa) and the result oriented vehicle (phalavajrayana, 'Bras-Bu sNgags-Kyi Theg-Pa)." Thus all dharma systems are encompassed within these two, the sutras and the tantras. Due to its many special features, the tantric Vidyadharayana which uses the result ('Bras-Bu)[6] is superior to the sutra path which focuses on the causes of gaining enlightenment.

The Differences between Sutra and Tantra

According to the sutra system of the causal vehicle relying on external characteristics (rGyu'i mTshan-Nyid-Kyi Theg-Pa), the basic nature (Khams, root component) of the primordial ground heart of Buddhahood (sugatasara, Ye-gZhi bDe-gShegs sNying-Po) has from the beginning been possessed in seed-form by all sentient beings. Then due to the causal factor (rKyen) of the gradual development of both the accumulation of merit based on perceiving objects (dMigs-bCas bSod-Nams-Kyi Tshogs) and the accumulation of intrinsic knowing based on the non-perception of substantial objects (dMigs-Med Ye-Shes-Kyi Tshogs), at some time in the future, after a very long time at the end of three or seven or thirty-two immeasurable aeons (*bsKal-Pa Grangs-Med*), they will gain the stage of the result of Buddhahood. Therefore it is said that in this case the cause comes first and the result follows later.

According to the tantric system, the indestructible secret mantra vehicle (*guhyamantravajrayana, gSang-sNgags rDo-rJe Theg-Pa*), the ground essence of natural clarity[7] has all good qualities (*Yon-Tan*) effortlessly arising (*Lhun-Grub*) and is present in one's own mind. Like the sky it is the ground on which the cleaning is done[8]. On top of that is that which is to be purified (*sByang-Bya*), the afflictions (*Nyon-Mongs*) of the eight consciousnesses (*Tshogs-brGyad*)[9] with their objects, which are like clouds arising in the sky. The agents of purification (*sByong-Bar-Byed-Pa*) are the profound methods of the ripening initiations and the liberating developing (*bsKyed-Rim*) and perfecting (*rDzogs-Rim*) systems by which the obscurations are quickly cleared away just as the wind clears away the clouds in the sky. The result of this cleansing (*sByang-'Bras*) is that one gains the Buddha's stage of the clear understanding of the original nature of the ground of all (*alayavijñāna, Kun-gZhi*), the primordial ground heart of Buddhahood (*bDe-gSheg-sNying-Po*). This is gained quickly, either in this life, in the bardo intermediate stage after death, or at the longest after seven lives. Since this doctrine has the power to accomplish this it is said to have the nature of the non-difference of cause and effect (*rGyu-'Bras dByer-Med*). Therefore although the sutra and tantra have the same intention, which is the attainment of the result of buddhahood, their methods of practice are different.

Those who practise the sutra path are ignorant of their original nature which is the great even openness of the natural non-duality of the appearances of samsara and of the naturally perfectly pure mandala of the meditation deities[10]. Due to this they have the view of adopting [virtue] and abandoning [sin] whereas tantricas have the knowledge inseparable from the truth of the pure equality of all things, and so, being able to practise the non-duality of cause and effect and of adopting and abandoning, they are not ignorant of the correct view.

In the sutra system there is the concept (*dMigs*) of adopting and abandoning and so one is not able to use all things as aids on the path. But in the tantric system there are many different methods of practising according to the result which is thereby quickly gained and so it is more profound. Due to this, tantra has the way of practice that is free of difficulties (*dKa'-Tshegs-Med*) while the sutra path lacks this quality. This deep way is only for those with very sharp intellects for only they can do it fully and so this tantric path is very special.

Moreover this non-difference of cause and result is clear in the *Anuttarayoga* system and is supremely present in the great completion (*rDzogs-Pa Chen-Po*) free of all worldly activity and effort. Also, compared with the sutra system, kriyayoga and so forth are also more free of ignorance[11] and so are special. And with the six classes of tantra[12], if the first ones are compared with the later ones then the latter will be seen to be higher (*Ma-rMongs*, less dull) and therefore special.

Therefore the sutra way is known as the causal vehicle (*rGyu'i-Theg-Pa*). By the practice of its path which is the cause of Buddhahood, the result is gained later. In tantra, however, by means of the supreme method, by using the path of the result of the three modes of enlightenment (*kāya*, *sKu*), the result is gained very quickly and so it is called the result vehicle (*'Bras-Bu'i-Theg-Pa*).

Nyingma System of Tantra

Now although there are countless tantras in the Tibetan system, they can be distinguished as to whether they are from the old or new translation period and so we have these two classes, the new translations (*Phyi-'Gyur*) and the old translations (*sNga-'Gyur*, or *rNying-Ma*).

Regarding the doctrines of the old translation school, THE EXPLANATORY TANTRA: ASSEMBLY OF CLARITY (*bShad-rGyud dGongs-Pa 'Dus-Pa*), which is regarded as being authentic by all the Tibetan Buddhists, says, "Kun-'Byung-'Dren Dang dKa'-Thub Rigs dBang-bsGyur Thabs-Kyi Theg-Pao." That is, "There are the three Dharma vehicles, namely *Kun-'Byung-'Dren*, *dKa'-Thub Rigs*, and *dBang-bsGyur-Thabs*."[13] Of the paths of sutra and tantra, the tantric paths are more powerful. In particular the *dBang-bsGyur Thabs-Kyi Theg-Pa* (*shaktiupayayana*, vehicle of powerful means) is special because the tantras of the three lower classes[14] employ the encouraging (*bLang*) of virtues and inhibiting (*Dor*) of stains (*Dri-Ma*) of the mind (*Khams*) and this is very difficult and tiring.

The View of Mahayoga

Yet, in fact, this effort is not necessary for *uttpanna mahayoga* teaches that from or on or in (*Las*) all-encompassing space (*dharmadhātu, dByings*) inseparable from primordial awareness[15] (*Rig-Pa*) free of all change, all phenomena[16] are the energy flow of awareness[17] and thus from the very beginning there has been exactly and only Buddhahood (*mNgon-Par Byang-Chub-Pa*).

The View of Anuyoga

This is the view that all memories and thoughts, whatever arises in the mind (*Dran-Rig*), have been Buddha (*Sang-rGyas* i.e. pure and perfect) from the very beginning within the great expanse of clarity (*dharmadhātu, 'Od-gSal Yangs-Pa Chen-Po*).

The View of Atiyoga

The effortful practice of causes and conditions[18] is not necessary since in just this present awareness (*vidya, Rig-pa*) the three modes or kāyas[19] are naturally complete and by knowledge of this crucial point one has the purity which is totally free of samsara. This is the view of the Mahasampanna or Mahasandi, *rDzogs-Pa-Chen-Po*, Atiyoga.

Mahasampanna atiyoga has the three aspects of *Sems-sDe* (*cittavarga*), *kLong-sDe* (*khavarga*) and *Man-Ngag-sDe* (*upadeshvarga*).

Regarding the view of *Sems-sDe*, the mind section, whatever appears[20] is seen to be within the nature of the mind[21] and that mind itself[22] arises as self-existing or naturally occurring intrinsic knowing (*Rang-Byung-Gi Ye-Shes*). Therefore there is not anything other than this self-existing intrinsic knowing and so one must enter the clarity (*gTan-La 'Bebs-Pa*) of this subject (*Yul-Can*[23], the one who 'has' the object) in the situation of the primordial purity (*Ka-Dag*) of open awareness, vidya and śūnyatā (*Rig-sTong*).

The system of teaching for this path has certain similarities with Mahamudra (*Phyag-Chen*). However the Mahamudra practice is to understand the nature of the object (*Yul-La Phar-rGyas 'Debs-Pa*) whereas this *Sems-sDe* system concentrates on understanding the nature of the subject (*Yul-Can*), and so they are not the same.

Regarding the view of the space section, *kLong-sDe*, all possible phenomena (*dharmas, Chos*) have no other place or destination than to be within the nature of dharmatā samantabhadra (*Chos-Nyid Kun-Tu-bZang-Po,* that is the actuality of perfection within the dharmadhātu). Therefore since there is no other source (*gZhan-'Byung 'Gog-Pa*) than the nature (*kLong-Las,* from within) of dharmatā [the actuality of existence] we relax to find ourselves within the situation free of effort (*Bya-rTsol-Med-Pa*) which is the very important and essential point of freedom from forcing subject on to object[24]. By means of this, one has the intrinsic knowing of the inseparability (*Zung-'Jug*) of depth and clarity (*śūnyatā prakash, Zab-gSal*). This is the profound method for practising the 'rainbow body' (*indradhanurupa, 'Ja'-Lus*) and the indestructible mode (*vajrakāya, rDo-rJe'i-sKu*). All the Vidyadharas (*Rig-'Dzin*) who formerly entered on this tantric path gained the rainbow body (*jñānakāya, Ye-Shes-Kyi sKu*).

This kLong-sDe path of the arising of vital clarity (*'Od-gSal rTsis-Po Cir-Byad-Pa*) seems to resemble the five stages (*pancakrama, Rim-lNga*) of the Guhyasamaja teachings of the New Translation Schools. Yet with the *pancakrama,* the activities of the five winds (*vayu, rLung*) are bound and by this important step the illusory body, the reflected image of form, is firmly held. Then, following from this, one gains the brilliance of clarity [i.e. one gains a light body]. Thus this method requires effort. But *kLong-sDe* is free of any forcing of subject onto object (*dMigs-gTad Bral-Ba*) and so it keeps the mind in the situation free of effort and striving, and therefore these two methods are not the same.

Regarding the view of Man-Ngag-Gi-sDe (*upadeshvarga*), by the non-dual intrinsic knowing of union (*yuganadha, Zung-'Jug,* full coupling of appearances and śūnyatā, etc.) free of adopting and discarding (*sPang-bLang*) all the phenomena of samsara and nirvana are practised or experienced (*sKyel-Ba*) within the situation of actuality, dharmatā, that is not grasped at as mere emptiness[25]. By this essential point (*gNad,* vital idea or understanding) samsara and nirvana are seen to be without any difference as awareness (*Rig-Pa*) itself alone. The dharmatā object arises clearly in mind and then one's own awareness (*vidya, Rig-Pa*) matures with the continuous linking of the emergence of the field[26]. All examining and discriminating (*Yid-dPyod*) ceases and one comes to clearly experience the natural clarity of the original mode (*gNas-Lugs*)[27].

By this view of *gMan-Ngag sDe* the vision (*sNang-Ba*) of the direct path (*Thod-rGal*) is made key. It may seem similar to the New Translation doctrine of *sByor-Drug* but with the *sByor-Drug* the five winds (*rLung-lNga*) are forced into the central channel, *avadhuti*, and by this important point, by means of making effort the appearances of śūnyatā's form are caused to arise and thus one slowly advances on the path of great bliss (*mahasukha, bDe-Ba Chen-Po*). Whereas here with *Man-Ngag-sDe*, mental examining and discrimination are abandoned and then one is clearly present with the natural clarity of the original mode – and so these two methods are not similar.

This path of *Man-Ngag-sDe* is superior to the practice of liberation in the *jñānakāya indradhanurupa* (*Ye-Shes-Kyi-sKu-'Ja'-Lus*) of *kLong-sDe* and so on, for here there are not even the pure traces of the fine and pure body that is developed from the rough forms of body, speech and mind[28]. But here with the full development of the non-dual arising (*sNang-Ba*, vision, experience) of the complete liberation of both object and subject (*Chos-Nyid Zad-Pa*), all the rough and fine aspects of body, speech and mind come within the situation of the modes of enlightenment (kāyas), and intrinsic knowing (*jñāna*) (*sKu-Dang Ye-Shes*) and without any false ground (*gZhi-Med* i.e. without ignorance, *avidya*, or the ground consciousness, *alayavijñāna*), awareness, vidya, becomes completely free and pure.

Now we shall consider why these three, *Sems-sDe, kLong-sDe* and *Man-Ngag-sDe* are called *rDzog-Pa-Chen-Po* (*Mahasampanna*, 'Great Completion'). This is because all phenomena, the entities (*Chos*) that compose all the possible existences and appearances (*sNang-Srid*) of samsara and nirvana[29], are completely or fully (*rDzog-Pa*)[30] within this awareness emptiness (*vidya śūnyatā, Rig-sTong*) and so it is *rDzog-Pa* or *sampanna* or complete. And there is no other method superior to this for giving release from samsara and so it is great, *Chen-Po* or *maha*.

The original situation (*Thog-Ma'i gNas-Lugs*, the natural uncontrived as-it-isness), the ground (*gZhi*) of unborn śūnyatā, has the actual nature (*Ngo-Bo*, like the sky) of the primordial purity of the inseparability of awareness and śūnyatā (*Ka-Dag-Gi Rig-sTong dByer-Med*). Śūnyatā's radiance[31] is unceasing. From śūnyatā the natural quality (*Rang-bZhin*, own face) effortlessly arises as whatever can possibly appear (*Thams-Cad*, here this means *Ci-Shar*) and this is the inseparability of clarity and śūnyatā (*gSal-sTong dByer-Med*). The energy flow or wave (*rTsal*)[32] of that shining void awareness manifests as whatever might arise, both pure and impure (*Dag Ma-Dag*)[33] and this is all pervading compassion (*Thug-rJe Kun-Khyab*) or the inseparability of appearance and emptiness (*sNang-sTong dByer-Med*).

The difference between ordinary mind (*citta, Sems*), and natural awareness (*vidya, Rig-Pa*) will now be shown. Due to the power of ignorance[34] there occur the suddenly arising thoughts (*gLo-Bur-Gyi rNam-rTog*) of many different memories and apprehensions[35] and this is called 'ordinary mind'[36]. By the power of not entering upon this deception of ignorance, mind is free of the relative notions[37] of graspable object and grasping mind (*gZung-'Dzin*) and is also free of the relative position of the non-grasping of clarity and śūnyatā[38] and so recognises that the empty śūnyatā nature of that freedom from grasping is clarity and emptiness. This is what is known as awareness (*vidya, Rig-Pa*).

The aspect of appearance (*sNang-Ba'i Cha*) of the forms of karma[39] in the mind is samsara (*'Khor-Ba*). Mind's true nature is śūnyatā and that is nirvana (*Myang-'Das*). In the natural situation (*Ngang*) of the void true nature of mind itself (*Sems-Nyid, i.e. Rig-Pa*) there is no ground for making any difference (*dBye-rGyu-Med*) between samsara and nirvana and so nirvana and samsara are without difference (*dByer-Med*).

See clearly (*Thag-bCad*) that what is seen (*sNang-Ba*) is mind. See clearly that mind is śūnyatā. See clearly that śūnyatā is fully joined with everything in complete non-duality. Then you will clearly know all phenomena (*Chos*) as awareness and śūnyatā (*Rig-sTong*). By practising in this way one will gradually come to recognise awareness and meditate on it by progressive stages.

To have mind's nature shown by the Guru and then clearly see all that arises to be awareness and śūnyatā is the immediate recognition of awareness (*Rig-Pa*). If one does not clearly understand awareness and śūnyatā in this life yet, due to the power of one's meditation, recognition arises while one is in the bardo (*Bar-Do*, intermediate state before the next birth), then this is *Thod-rGal* or direct recognition of awareness (*Thod-rGal-Ba'i Rig-Pa Rang-Ngo 'Phrod-Pa'i Tshad*).

In brief, one's own mind is at this very moment stainless clarity and śūnyatā free of grasping, so, for whatever thoughts or ideas stay or move due to lack of proper control[40], do not react in terms of good and bad, inhibiting and encouraging (dGag-bsGrub) and so on, but clearly maintain awareness and emptiness. The meditation method of this path is the supreme essential teaching.

Thus as Mahacharya Padmasambhava says in the fourth chapter of THE SEVEN CHAPTERED PRAYER (gSol-'Debs Le'u bDun-Ma):

"As regards the eye's objects which are the appearances of absolutely all the outer and inner entities which constitute the universe and its inhabitants, maintain the openness of allowing these appearances to arise yet without grasping at them as being something inherently real. See that they are the radiant forms of clarity and emptiness, pure and naturally free from graspable objects and grasping mind.

As regards the ear's objects of the sounds which are held to as being pleasant or unpleasant, for all sounds maintain the openness of sound and emptiness free of all involved discriminating thought. This is sound and emptiness, the unborn and unobstructed Buddhas' speech.

As regards the objects of our mentation, the restless movement of the five afflicting poisons'[41] thoughts, do not enter upon the intellect's artificial activities of awaiting future thoughts and following after past thoughts. By leaving the restless movement as it is, we are liberated in the Dharmakaya.

Outwardly, see that all the appearances of graspable objects are pure. Inwardly, experience the liberation of your grasping mind. With this non-duality of outer and inner, experience the clarity of seeing your own nature."

The ground (gZhi), path (Lam), and result ('Bras-Bu)

The Ground

The original natural mode [of awareness, *Rig-Pa*] is not touched by all that appears as samsara and nirvana and it is not affected by the rust of confusion. The unaltered [*rJen-Pa*, raw or naked] natural mode never experiences confusion and never experiences dualistic thoughts. It is not built up by anything whatsoever that might occur (*Cir Yang Ma-Grub*)[42] and it does not become a cause for anything (*Cir-Yang Byung-Du Ma-bTub-Pa*)[43]. This is known as the ground (*gZhi*).

The Path

When this present mind (*Da-lTa'i Rig-Pa*) is kept relaxed, this open empty clarity free of good thoughts, bad thoughts, and neutral thoughts (*Lung Ma-bsTan*) is like the centre of the clear sky and that is the path.

The Result

All the good qualities of the path become manifest and ignorance and confusion are purified in their own place and then the dharmadhātu (*Chos-Kyi dByings*) becomes clearly evident. This is considered to be the result.

Moreover this is both the view of the profound primordial purity (*Ka-Dag*) of the cutting through (*Khregs-Chod*) path and the view of the vast effortless arising (*Lhun-Grub*) of the spontaneous (*Thod-rGal*) path.

Regarding primordial purity, the original ground (*Thog-Ma'i-gZhi*) where no beings have arisen due to confusion and no Buddhas have arisen due to the absence of confusion[44], is the true nature of one's own awareness which from the very beginning has been free of the fault of obscurations and so is primordially pure. Therefore that ground of all sentient beings abides as primordial Buddhahood[45] and this is known as 'natural mode always good', *Chos-sKu Kun-Tu bZang-Po* (*Dharmakāya Samantabhadra*) or as 'Great Mother transcendent wisdom natural mode', *Yum-Chen Phar-Phyin Chos-Kyi-sKu* (*Prajnaparamita Dharmakāya*).

Due to not recognising this original ground and not understanding it, the three ignorances[46] and the six consciousnesses [of the five senses and of mentation] develop and so from the cause of the twelve factors of dependent co-arising[47] (pratityasamutpada, rTen-'Brel bCu-gNyis) there comes the future impure karmic activity due to which beings wander among the appearances of the six realms of samsara.

In that way all the emanations (Chos-'Phrul, magical illusory forms) of the ground radiance or vision (gZhi-sNang) arise without actually wavering from the nature of the ground itself. Furthermore these ideas or images or experiences (sNang-Ba) are mere appearance devoid of any inherent substance or existence (Don-La Ma-Grub-Pa) and are only the forms and situations of appearance and emptiness (sNang-sTong).

The true nature (Ngo-Bo) of the ground is not touched by any aspect of samsara or nirvana and so it is empty (sTong-Pa). Its natural quality (Rang-bZhin) abides as perfect clarity while the energy flow (Thug-rJe) comes out as whatever can possibly arise, and so mind abides as unobstructed clarity. Thus the ground has the nature of these three aspects of true nature, natural quality, and energy flow, and whatever sudden thoughts, good and bad, arise and are liberated, these make not the slightest benefit or harm for awareness (Rig-Pa). Therefore without bias or partiality, just as a sesame seed is full of oil, awareness pervades all the hosts of thoughts that arise from mind's energy (rTsal) and catches them immediately[48].

Yet all the contrived aspects of the suddenly arising ground of all ignorance (gLo-Bur Kun-gZhi Ma-Rig-Pa) cover the face of the uncontrived primordially present (Ye-Babs) Dharmakāya, and then one is made to wander in samsara. So no matter what afflictions (Nyon-Mongs) or thoughts arise, do not believe in them or rely on them. It is not enough just to stay with recognition of the arising of thoughts. No matter what thoughts arise one must maintain the original unchanging intrinsic knowing (Ye-Shes) free of objects and supports, the very direct (Zang-Thal-Med[49]) intrinsic knowing free of all relative positions (sPros-Bral). If one remains like that, then, when movement and restless disturbance come again like water descending from a high mountain, one will not go seeking after outer objects. Within one will not go under the power of grasping. So without doing anything artificial, again and again one must maintain the very clear experience of the original situation which is not adulterated or touched by anything whatsoever of the unrelaxed contrived mental discriminations of thoughts arising (*sPro*) and ceasing (*bsDu*). It is necessary to keep ceaselessly to this practice for a long time.

If one is able to maintain this practice, then with just this awareness (*Rig-Pa*) itself there is the primordial presence of the three modes of enlightenment [natural, enjoyment, manifest; Dharmakāya, Sambhogakāya, Nirmanakāya] and the primordial completion of the two accumulations [of merit and wisdom] as its own character or share (*Rang-Chas*, 'one's own portion'). Therefore by this essential point of being untouched by the adventitious features of inhibiting and encouraging, accepting and rejecting, and by all the phenomena (*Chos*) of cause and effect, the good qualities of study and practice, comprising all the meditative experiences arising with intrinsic knowing, such as happiness (*bDe*), clarity (*gSal*) and non-mentation (*Mi-rTog*) will arise and grow easily and without effort.

Therefore whatever experiences arise, whether good or bad, sickness or health, joy or sorrow, hopes or doubts and so forth, do not go after them, do not put yourself under their power. You must deeply and directly experience your own unchanging original nature (*gNyug-Ma'i Rang-Zhal*). Then by simply keeping to this without moving after anything else, by knowing this one point all will be freed. Knowing one and freeing all is the all-sufficient, all-inclusive profound doctrine, and it is most important and wonderful.

NOTES

[1] That is reflection on the eighteen factors of the freedoms and opportunities (*Dal-'Byor*) of a precious human birth (*Mi-Lus-Rin-Po-Che*); death and impermanence (*'Chi-Ba Mi-rTag-Pa*); karmic causes and consequences (*Las-rGyu-'Bras*); the sufferings of samsara (*'Khor-Ba' Nyes-dMigs*). See Low, J. SIMPLY BEING, (CPI Antony Rowe, November 2010), Chapter 1.

[2] Suffering, the causes of suffering, the ending of suffering, and the path towards that which is the eight-fold way ('Phags-Pa'i-Lam Yan-Lag brGyad) consisting of right view, right understanding, right speech, right activity, right livelihood, right effort, right recollection, and right meditation.

[3] That is morality, absorbed contemplation, and wise discernment.

[4] Generosity, morality, patience, diligence, mental stability, wise discernment.

[5] Giving whatever is necessary, speaking sweetly, acting correctly and without hypocrisy, acting for the benefit of beings.

[6] That is, the natural situation.

[7] gZhi Rang-bZhin 'Od-gSal-Ba'i sNying-Po, which is Ye-gZhi bDe-gShegs sNying-Po.

[8] sByang gZhir-Byas, i.e. it is the pure object on which the 'dust' seems to gather.

[9] That is, the five sense consciousnesses, mental consciousness (Yid-Kyi rNam-Par-Shes-Pa), the mental consciousness of the afflictions (Nyon-Mongs-Kyi Yid-Kyi rNam-Par-Shes-Pa), and the 'ground of all' consciousness (Kun-gZhi rNam-Par-Shes-Pa).

[10] Which is the understanding possessed by the practitioners of tantra.

[11] Ma-rMongs, i.e. are nearer the actual truth.

[12] Bya-rGyud, sPyod-rGyud, rNal-'Byor-rGyud, Pha-rGyud, Ma-rGyud, gNyis-Med-rGyud.

[13] Sarvabhavanayakayana or Kun-'Byung-'Dren refers to the vehicle of listeners (Śrāvakayana, Nyan-Thos Kyi Theg- Pa) and the vehicle of the isolated awakeners (pratyekabuddhayana, Rang-rGyal-Kyi Theg-Pa) and the vehicle of the enlightened altruistic ones (bodhisattvayana, Byang-Chub Sems-dPa'i Theg-Pa). The tapasvinkulayana or dKa'-Thub Rigs refers to the vehicle of activity (kriyayana, Bya-rGyud) and the vehicle of conduct (caryayana, sPyod-rGyud) and the vehicle of yogis (anuttarayana, rNal-'Byor-rGyud). The shak-tiupayayana or dBang-bsGyur Thabs-Kyi Theg-Pa refers to the father tantras (pitryogayana, Pha-rGyud) [mahayoga], and the mother tantras (matrayo-gayana, Ma-rGyud) [anuyoga], and the non-dual tantras (advayayogayana, gNyis-Med rGyud) [atiyoga].

[14] rGyud-sDe gSum, that is Bya-rGyud, sPyod-rGyud, rNal-'Byor -rGyud.

[15] gZhi-rDzog, the natural ground in which all is contained; it is pure vidya or awareness itself.

[16] Chos, dharmas, whatever is possible anywhere in samsara or nirvana.

[17] Rig-Pa'i-rTsal; gSal-sTong gNyis-Med.

[18] rGyu-rKyen, here this implies bsKyed-Rim and rDzog-Rim.

[19] Dharmakaya, Sambhogakaya, Nirmanakaya, these three constitute the natural mode of Buddhahood.

[20] *Cir-sNang*, this means all the possible objects of the six senses.

[21] *Sems-Kyi Ngo-Bor-sNang-Ba-Yin* i.e. whatever they are for you is something that your own mind identifies; all you ever have is your own experience, the appearances of both self and other, subject and object, which arise from your mind's true nature.

[22] Cittata, *Sems-Nyid*, the 'basic' mind itself, free of obscuration and artifice.

[23] Here *Yul-Can* indicates *Sems-Nyid*, as both are inseparable from the ground.

[24] *dMigs-gTad-Bral-Ba*, just as when familiar footsteps are recognised one does not have to wonder or worry who is there.

[25] *sTong-'Dzin Dang Bral-Ba*, i.e. not believing in just empty sunyata but seeing the open aware dimension in which all that is possible arises.

[26] *Lug-Gu rGyud-Kyi-sKu*, like a row of sheep one after the other, or like beads moving on the thread of a rosary, so that awareness is affected neither by samsara or nirvana.

[27] The uncontrived changeless pattern of actuality.

[28] By means of *kLong-sDe* the rough physical form is transformed into a fine light body yet there still remain traces of the *Shes-Bya sGrib-Pa*, the subtle traces remaining after the removal of the power of the afflictions, kleshas, *Nyon-Mongs*.

[29] Which are all the possibilities that there ever can be.

[30] On a general level all objects are defined and held in place by mind. Mind says, "It is a table" but the table never says, "I am a table." Mind creates all the appearances that can be known. They are all within that mind and whatever they are when that mind does not consider them, they are certainly not any 'thing' – for that is already a concept from mind.

[31] *mDangs*, natural glow or expression, like the spreading of the dawn.

[32] Like the heat and light of the sun's rays.

[33] Pure and impure as discriminated as existing in truth by ordinary beings.

[34] Avidya, *Ma-Rig-Pa*, nescience, forgetting the true nature; being intoxicated by what is occurring so that what is occurring is taken to be self-existing with the consequence of forgetfulness or ignoring of the actual non-duality of event and ground.

[35] *Dran-Pa* i.e. many false ideas arise as when one mistakes a rope for a snake on a dark night.

[36] *Sems* here meaning *Yid* or manas, mental consciousness, mentation. There do not seem to be any words in English which can precisely show the subtle

uses of these words. On other occasions *Sems* is used in the sense of *Sems-Nyid*, the mind itself free of artifice.

[37] Aparapanca, *sPros-Bral*, absence of conceptual elaboration, i.e. not relying on dualistic concepts such as beginning and ending, coming and going etc.

[38] By not grasping at this clarity of appearance but seeing that it is empty, there is no basis from which false dual notions can arise, such as believing that nirvana is better than samsara, and thus one is bound neither by the iron chain of grasping nor by the golden chain of clarity.

[39] *Las-Kyi rNam-Pa*, whatever is seen, all the appearances of karma's result, i.e. the six realms.

[40] *Kha-Yan-Du kLod*, like a careless mother allowing her children to do whatever they like, or like continuing to use a machine even after it is broken. Control here does not refer to dualistic control of subject over object, but to the effortless 'control' of relaxing and integrating whatever arises in the space of awareness.

[41] Anger, desire, stupidity, pride, jealousy.

[42] i.e. never becomes false and artificial.

[43] It is not a raw material like iron ore which can be made into many different things.

[44] That is, it is like a lump of silver which has not been made into a pot or other object, and has also not gone back to being ore mixed with earth – it is open potentiality.

[45] *Ye-Ne Sangs-rGyas* i.e. they have always and inalienably had Buddha nature. *Sangs* means pure and free of all faults, and *rGyas* means having all good qualities naturally present.

[46] Co-emergent ignorance (*Lhan-Cig-sKyes-Pa'i Ma-Rig-Pa*), discriminating ignorance (*Kun-Tu-brTags-Pa'i Ma-Rig-Pa*), and ignorance of being blind to karma (*Las-rGu-'Bras-La-Mongs-Pa'i Ma-Rig-Pa*).

[47] Ignorance (*Ma-Rig-Pa*); habitual tendencies (*'Du-Byed*); consciousness (*rNam-Shes*); name and form (*Ming Dang gZugs*); the six activity fields of the eye, ear, nose, tongue, body and intellect (*sKye-mChed Drug*); contact (*Reg-Pa*); feeling (*Tshor-Ba*); craving (*Sred-Pa*); attachment (*Len-Pa*); rebirth (*Srid-Pa*);birth (*sKye-Ba*); old age and death (*rGa-Shi*).

[48] Just as the sky 'catches' or contains all the sun's rays, awareness 'catches' the thoughts by showing their non-duality – all appearance is inseparable from awareness which is inseparable from ground emptiness.

[49] here *Med* does not signify a negative.

3

Bardo Instructions Radiating Clarity Like the Sun

From the terma of Nuden Dorje Dropen Lingpa Drolo Tsal
called
THE PROFOUND MEANING OF THE INDESTRUCTIBLE ESSENCE,
a text belonging to the dzogchen series:
THE VIEW OF INFINITE WISDOM OF THE PEACEFUL
AND WRATHFUL DEITIES

Salutation to our own awareness, the Guru Kuntu Zangpo.

Regarding these instructions which directly introduce yogis to the bardos, bardo indicates an interlude, an intermission, a moment or period occurring between other, different, moments or periods.

Those who seek to recognise themselves and to work for the benefit of others but who are without these teachings are impoverished, as are their students.

Six bardos are described in this text: the bardos of the nature of birth; of dream; of meditation; of death; of actuality and of becoming. This text is the actual essence of all the instructions on the bardo.

The Dharma King Trisong Detsen (*Khri Srong lDeu bTsan*) asked the great master Padmasambhava,"Please, give me a clear instruction on the meaning of the bardos."

The Guru replied from his heart, "Listen dharma king. There are six bardos.

The **FIRST IS THE BARDO OF BIRTH** which goes from the time of entering your mother's womb, through birth, until you come to your death. At first everything is confusing and then happiness and sorrow start to be differentiated. The body is like a house, and the mind is like a house owner. If this is realised then the mind is seen very clearly. If it is not realised then one is bewildered and all the causes of samsara are collected.

In the middle of our heart is our precious mind (*citta*) at the centre of the eight corners of the heart channel. Here awareness arises clearly and without attachment. For example, it is like a lamp shining in a pot. This is called the lamp of the flesh heart (*Tsit-Ta Sha-Yi sGron-Ma*). Self-manifesting and uncontrived, it abides in the heart channel.

Its expression is the spheres of light arising within this expanse of wisdom within which the forty-two peaceful gods reside in the heart. Due to this, the blazing wrathful gods arise at the top of the head. These peaceful and wrathful forms are the manifestation of the energy of awareness. For example, it is like a lamp in a pot which has a raised lid letting light shine out. Ah! How this clarity appears is your own experience.

On the basis of this, light radiates as large and small spheres (*Thig-Le*) and as rainbow light leading to the arising of many divine mandalas. The condition giving rise to this is the channel connecting the eye to the heart. It is narrow at the bottom and wide at the top, shaped like a cow's horn. It is free of blood and lymph and so is empty and clear. Being connected to the eyeball, it is the basis for seeing both the qualities and faults of appearances. This is called the lamp of the channel of white soft silk (*rTsa Dar-dKar Lam-Kyi sGron-Ma*).

When that is connected with the eyeball, there is the path of awareness where wisdom unceasingly separates samsara and nirvana. This is called the lamp of water which sees or lassoes at a distance (*rGyang-Zhag Chu'i sGron-Ma*). Its outer object is the sky, infinite spaciousness free of all contrivance. Within it is unchanging wisdom, the purity of awareness and emptiness.

With the non-duality of emptiness and wisdom within the infinity of space, wisdom ceaselessly manifests as spheres of light. This is the lamp of the spheres of light of emptiness (*Thig-Le sTong-Pa'i sGron-Ma*). It is like a peacock's feather, a rainbow, or light from a crystal.

The rainbow coloured light arises in a shape like the vowel sign naro ⌣. This is called the pure lamp of emptiness and wisdom, in which emptiness and wisdom are non-dual and arise without effort. This is called the lamp of self-arising wisdom (*Shes-Rab Rang-Byung-Gi sGron-Ma*).

At first, Buddhas and sentient beings were not different. Kuntu-zangpo gained buddhahood without having performed any virtuous actions. Sentient beings became bewildered due to their own nature without having performed any unvirtuous actions. Buddhas' aware-ness naturally sees with the view that understands the production of thought. They do not use the winds of karma and so do not collect the causes of samsara. Being free of graspable objects and grasping minds operating within or without, they actualise their own awareness. They see this awareness, this wisdom which is without root or base. The minds of sentient beings become bewildered with the duality of outer graspable objects and inner grasping mind. Bewildered by the unpredictable habits of the ground of all, confused sentient beings do not see their own actuality.

If natural understanding is clearly actualised then clarity is unceasing like the rising sun. Awareness, free of thoughts, is self-manifesting and graspable objects and grasping mind are purified. This is the understanding of the bardo of birth.

The **SECOND BARDO IS THE BARDO OF DREAMS** which occurs when the appearances of the waking day cease. Then, while sleeping at night, karmic traces cause the bewilderment of dreams. If you recognise this, then the ceaseless flow of appearances arising from the consciousness which is the ground of all melts into the awareness in the centre of the heart and completely merges with the sleep free of all memories and traces whatsoever. This is like the sky, a clarity free of grasping. This is called the ground clarity. It is also known as the meeting of the mother and son actualities. Because of it, wisdom arises to itself.

If at the beginning, people do not recognise the nature of their dreams, then in the hollow channels in the four directions in the heart, and in their interstices, and above and below, the wind energy and the mind go to the various channels in the lungs and heart. Due to this, many different magical forms of gods and demons arise. If the wind-mind descends down the hollow channels, there is a feeling of everything falling as in a landslide, and it is dark and one experiences the suffering of the hell, hungry ghost, animal realms and so forth.

In the separate channels of the six senses, images arise of the objects pertaining to each of them. Confused appearances arise in dreams from the operation of tsan demons in the lung channel, gyalpo demons in the heart channel, mamo demons in the liver and kidney channels, dud and the'u-rang demons in the stomach channel, and sadag demons in the intestine channel. If the wind mind enters any of the channels, then by understanding or not understanding their nature, the yogi's body does not or does become full of worldly appearances and the sufferings of samsara – and that is what she or he dreams. It is very important to practise being aware of dreaming, purifying dreaming, and resting in natural clarity.

THIRDLY, understanding THE BARDO OF MEDITATION. When practising focused meditation on the forms of the deities one needs a clarity free of grasping and conceptual judgement towards these appearances. Abide in the situation of awareness that neither changes nor remains. Free of limits, the experience of the natural mode dharmakāya becomes clear, and with the non-duality of happiness and emptiness in the domain of the four joys, one remains undisturbed by thoughts or expression. Those who have awakened to this situation should not go after previous thoughts, nor wait on future events. The awareness that is present now, fresh, uncontrived, naturally effortless, completely free of encouraging or inhibition, this is the empty natural situation. It is free of the position of annihilation which craves emptiness. Free of all encouraging and inhibiting it is the empty natural situation. There is no other Buddha. One's own awareness is the Buddha. It is free of the limitations of effortful endeavour and attempts to abandon samsara. Sinking appears as the unwavering meditation of infinite spaciousness dharmadhātu. Excitation is the clarity of actuality, the highest view. Foggy stupidity is wisdom's self-perception arising for itself. Awareness is direct, without partiality and free of reificatory thought. This wisdom free of thought is mahamudra, the great givenness itself.

FOURTHLY, regarding the natural condition of THE BARDO OF DEATH, the bardo which lasts from the fatal sickness until the point of death. Even if one is without attachment to and longing for all the things that are dear to one, the illusions of wealth, possessions, country, friends and so forth, there is sorrow at one's own death and the fear of being alone. One feels sad when remembering the sins that one has previously performed. One is tormented by thinking of all the dharma that one has not done and that one must leave this world empty-handed. One's house might collapse, or be burned by fire. One might be carried away by water, or fall from a high place. Sorrow, fear and anguish without limit are the marks of death. At that time, yogis who meditate will maintain the radiance of awareness, clarity and emptiness unobscured. With that understanding they will experience the meaning of actuality. If you do not get that understanding it shows you have not been diligent and careful in your practice. So be careful and unwaveringly attentive.

FIFTHLY, regarding the natural condition of THE BARDO OF ACTUALITY, the outer appearance is like sunset, the inner appearance is dark and obscure, then clear appearances occur like early dawn in the morning. At that time yogis experience the bardo's confusion. Being free of a flesh body one moves without obstruction through hills and rocks, the peaceful and wrathful deities appear and the wisdom light, rays, colours arise in many different forms. Sounds, light and rays arise with large and small spheres (Thig-Le). At that time your own meditation deities will welcome you. You will experience unimpeded awareness free from encouraging and inhibiting, and be naturally free from benefit and harm, from hopes and fears.

SIXTH, regarding the natural condition of THE BARDO OF BECOMING, when one does not recognise the peaceful and wrathful gods of the bardo of actuality one is lost without place or direction. When the time comes to experience the happiness of the three upper realms [gods, demi-gods and humans] or the suffering of the three lower realms [animals, hungry ghosts and denizens of hells] according to the virtue or sin that one has acquired, the mind traverses the universe in an instant, moving rapidly here and there without intention or purpose. At that time it is vital to remember the mind's natural situation and to strongly enforce a connection with one's previous good actions.

Vajra Vows Seal Seal Seal[1]

From the time of birth until you are tormented by a fatal illness and your consciousness goes unconscious and wanders in the six realms, you wander here and there not serving your guru. Abandoning yourself, you do not attend to the teachings of the precious methods of enlightenment. In order to avoid that one needs the assistance given by visualising the three places of refuge with the devotion of understanding. Then, due to a shift created either by oneself or by the power of another, between inhaling and exhaling you should not doubt the natural clarity of the wisdom that arises for you. Then in the bardo of actuality you can see your own nature, the meeting of the mother and son aspects of emptiness and awareness. Therefore it is very important to practise clarity. If you see the meditation deities as you wander in the bardo of becoming, they will welcome you and guide you so that the bewildering appearances are purified in emptiness.

Vajra Vows

REGARDING THE BARDO OF BIRTH, you need a teaching to stop all doubts and uncertainties towards the outer and inner dharma teachings, an instruction that finds its way like a bird which never forgets its own nest.

REGARDING THE BARDO OF DREAMS, you need a teaching which shows how to inhibit the appearance of mental habits and their remnants and how to practise clarity and the union of emptiness and awareness, an instruction which is like a lamp placed in a dark room.

REGARDING THE BARDO OF MEDITATION, you need to see the actuality of your natural situation, the inseparability of emptiness and awareness. You need an instruction which is like a beautiful girl holding a mirror so that you can see your reflection.

REGARDING THE BARDO OF DEATH, you need to be certain of your own nature, not dispersing recollection or awareness but clarifying all that is unclear. For this you need an instruction like the letter of a king.

REGARDING THE BARDO OF ACTUALITY, for all appearances of whatever kind you need the faith and certain knowledge of the merging of awareness and appearance. For this you need an instruction that is like the meeting of mother and son.

REGARDING THE BARDO OF BECOMING, when there is the ripening of former actions one needs to be able to powerfully summon forth the results of former good actions. For this you need an instruction which is like a pipe repairing a broken canal.

Vajra Vows

Here is an explanation of THE EIGHTEEN WAYS OF CONSIDERING THE PROPERTIES OF THE SIX BARDOS. The eighteen are as follows: nature, name, differentiation, qualities, body [characteristics], duration, mode of appearance [examples], teaching [signs], practice, instructions, faults, benefits and establishment of boundaries and vows[2].

FIRST, THE NATURE OF ALL BARDOS

Present awareness is itself uncontrived and free of effortful activity. Flowing spontaneously, clarity and emptiness arise bright and fresh. If you do not actualise this you will wander in the bardos. But if you practise the actualisation of it you will be free of the bardos. Therefore keep your present awareness relaxed and uncontrived. Do not engage in artifice but remain fresh in your own place. This is the way to practise the nature of all the bardos.

Vajra Vows

SECOND, THE REASON WHY WE USE THE NAME OR WORD 'BARDO'

When all the appearances that arose as one's former habitual experience have stopped and the appearances that will be one's future habitual experience have not yet arisen, there is the in-between, that which is between the former and the future, and this is what the term 'bardo' generally implies. We can also indicate the specific meaning of each of the six types of 'bardo'.

Hence, *the bardo of birth* occurs once the body of one's previous life is left behind, and extends from the time of being in one's mother's womb until death. It includes all the appearances and confusing subtle ideas which occur in that period.

The bardo of dreams occurs when the experiences of yesterday have ended and the appearances of the next day are yet to occur. Between the day that has just passed and the day that will come next there occurs in deep unconscious sleep the habits which manifest as a false body. This is the confusion arising from perceptions and associations.

The bardo of meditation occurs when previously occurring ideas and events do not disturb and confusion about the future does not appear, so that one is fully present in one's natural situation and remains stable in natural clarity free of artifice.

The bardo of death occurs when the experiences of this life have ended and there occurs the fear that arises on the brink of death. One has to go to the place of one's next life and one is at the end of what is now one's previous life. There, between these two, one is not able to get rid of suffering.

The bardo of actuality arises and the appearances of sound, light and rays occur and through the fruits of one's practice, one experiences the happiness of actuality.

The bardo of becoming occurs when the experiences of actuality have ceased and the body of one's next life has not yet appeared. That place between is called 'becoming' because it is possible to enter the upper realms of happiness or the lower realms of woe. The full range of happiness and suffering is possible and so that stage is called the bardo of becoming.

Thus we have the names of the six bardos.   *Vajra Vows*

THIRD, THE DIFFERENTIATION OF THE BARDO INTO SIX

Firstly, *the bardo of birth* abides from birth for as long as one has not died.

Secondly, *the bardo of dreams* lies between the ending of the experiences of one day and the arising of the experiences of the next.

Thirdly, *the bardo of meditation* occurs between the clearing away of previous confusion and the arising of future confusion.

Fourthly, *the bardo of death*'s suffering occurs from the arrival of the fatal illness till the exit of the last breath.

Fifthly, *the bardo of actuality* with the peaceful and wrathful deities, occurs for the duration of the appearances of the peaceful and wrathful forms and their sound and light.

Sixthly, *the bardo of becoming* occurs during the confusion of the ripening of the effects of the actions that one has performed.

Vajra Vows

FOURTH, THE QUALITIES OF THE SIX BARDOS

To talk of the bardos as if they really exist is misleading because their quality is emptiness. However the mode of their appearance can be called 'bardo' according to the conventions of relative truth. But in the true nature, according to absolute truth, what is called 'bardo' does not exist. The outer appearances of forms, sounds, smells, tastes, sensations and phenomena do not endure for they cease and vanish. According to absolute truth, they lack even a hair's worth of true existence. Awakening to their absence of true existence is referred to as the 'outer emptiness'.

Within, the eyes, ears, nose, tongue, body and mentation are all in relative truth; they do not endure for they cease and vanish. According to absolute truth they lack even a dust-particle's worth of true existence. Awakening to their absence of true existence is referred to as the 'inner emptiness'.

The eighteen dhātus[3], the twelve partners[4] and all one's various inner ideas are all empty in their actual nature. All the dualities of outer objects and the subjects who know them are only the illusory forms of relative truth. In absolute truth they lack all real existence. By knowing the emptiness of outer and inner experience one knows that, in brief, all the phenomena of samsara and nirvana are empty. The quality of the bardo is emptiness.

Vajra Vows

FIFTH, THE CHARACTERISTICS OF THE BARDOS WILL BE SHOWN BY INDICATING THEIR PARTICULARITIES

The characteristic of the bardo of birth is that one's body is formed through the particular interaction of the five skandhas[5], the eighteen dhātus, the six sense organs and consciousnesses, the five sense organs, subject and object, and the afflictions and so on. The yogi who realises the illusory nature of these relative truth phenomena gains power over all that manifests.

The characteristic of the bardo of dreams is that during deep sleep there are present both the aspect of stupidity and the aspect of the evanescent quality of the display of the clarity of wisdom. While dreaming, appearances come and go and nothing is permanent. This illusory nature is the characteristic of the bardo of dreams.

The characteristic of the bardo of meditation is that all outer and inner phenomena have the nature of clarity and emptiness. This is the basis for the arising of the unification of calm abiding and insight, and of the developing stage of visualisation of deities and the completing stage of the primordial purity of the natural condition. This is the characteristic of the bardo of meditation.

The characteristic of the bardo of death is that a fatal illness occurs due to an imbalance in the elements. Body and mind separate and death begins. One has no power not to go and so one must go. One has no power to remain with friends, relations, possessions and countrymen and so one must go alone. But attachment, desire and longing continue and one is absorbed in worldly activities. Due to the power of previous involvements one has not believed the Dharma teachings on death, impermanence and so on and so one is involved and full of longing. One suffers from attachment to parents, children, relatives and friends. One's understanding becomes obscured and memory and knowledge become unreliable. These are the characteristics of the bardo of death.

The characteristic of the bardo of actuality is that the illusory form of the five skandhas dissolves, and flesh, blood, life force, breath, body and mind all separate. One manifests only the pure body of mental experience. The peaceful deities, the wrathful deities, lights, colours, spheres of light, small spheres, links of spheres, sounds, lights, rays – whatever occurs is the manifestation of one's own experience. The clarity aspect of wisdom is ceaseless and all manifestations have the quality of great happiness. In this pure infinity of great happiness whatever one experiences is the arising of the realm of actuality. This is the characteristic of the bardo of actuality.

The characteristic of the bardo of becoming is that one has separated from one's previous flesh and blood body and now has the illusory form created by mental activity. When the peaceful and wrathful forms arise from actuality one does not recognise the truth of that actuality. The deities, rays and five-coloured lights cause fear and trembling and one perceives them to be the enemy. Unable to grasp the nature of this revelation of actuality one is set travelling all over the place like a feather in the wind. Unable to settle anywhere, one's activity lacks purpose and direction. Like images in a dream the body is unable to stabilise itself for long and anger arises. The colours of the six realms, white, blue, and so on, arise in sequence. These experiences are the characteristics of the bardo of becoming.

Vajra Vows

SIXTH, THE DURATION OF THE BARDOS

The bardo of birth lasts from the time of entering one's mother's womb until the beginning of a mortal sickness.

The bardo of dreams continues from the time of entering deep sleep until one awakens.

The bardo of meditation endures for as long as one maintains awareness during even openness, between the ceasing of the previous thought and the arising of the next.

The bardo of death lasts from the time one is taken by a mortal illness until one's final breath is exhaled.

The bardo of actuality lasts from the final breath until the arising of spontaneous appearances.

The bardo of becoming lasts from the display of the peaceful and wrathful deities until one enters the womb.

These are the durations of the six bardos.   *Vajra Vows*

SEVENTH, ILLUSTRATING THE BARDOS BY THE USE OF EXAMPLES

In the bardo of birth the body and the mind are like a cairn and a bird. The body is gradually built up like a cairn. It is not known how long it will endure before destruction but it certainly has the nature of something that will be destroyed. The mind is like a bird on a cairn. It only rests there for a while before flying away, and it is not certain where it will go once it leaves. Likewise the mind does not remain in the corpse. The dead body is put somewhere but the mind wanders with no fixed direction. The voice, like the dragon's roar, does not last for long. Relatives come and take over the bird's nest, making themselves quite at home. But they do not remain together for long as they separate and spread out. Then they die one by one, passing away. Relatives are impermanent like the bird's nest, and partners certainly demonstrate impermanence. Just as the ploughman yokes cattle together, friends only stay together for a while before they go their own way. Life is like a stone rolling down a mountain without the power to stop itself. Similarly day by day, night by night, we move towards death. Possessions are like the bee's honey, we collect them ourselves but they end up being used by others.

The bardo of dreams is like an illusory form created by a magician. Nothing is really there but we see many things. Dreams seem to be real although they are mere appearances devoid of substance.

The bardo of meditation is like gazing gently at an open pasture. With relaxation and ease all difficulties and sorrows are calmed. Breathing gently, body and mind become happy. Due to the waves of samsaric confusion, one's body, voice and mind have been immersed in sorrow with no opportunity for happiness. With the instructions of one's teacher one's body, voice and mind relax and flow easily. With the even openness of meditation all the activities of one's body, like the easy movement of a wheel, flow peacefully without disturbance, twitching or irritation. One's voice becomes like the strings of a lute. The lute is able to make many different sounds but if the string is cut the flow of sound ceases. Similarly, with meditation, one speaks little nonsense. Resting in its own place one's voice is at ease. The mind is like a waterwheel; when the water stops, the wheel stops turning. Similarly, with meditation, thoughts and memories stop, as, without artifice, the mind is at ease with whatever occurs. That is an explanation of being at ease in body, voice and mind.

The bardo of death is like a person who has committed a crime and knows that they will suffer imprisonment. Although they know this they have no power to flee. They would like things to remain as they are but they are not able to maintain their situation and will be led away. Similarly, when the mortal sickness arrives, although one knows one is dying one has no power to resist it. One remembers all the sins that one has accumulated earlier in one's life and feels fear and dread but lacks any method to change things. One's house, property, wealth and possessions remain where they are and, separating from one's friends, one must go alone to wander in a land where everything is unknown. Thus the mind has to endure great suffering in the bardo of death.

The bardo of actuality is like being a single person who is surrounded by an army of a thousand soldiers. Wherever one looks there are peaceful and wrathful deities, lights, sounds, and rays in turbulent movement everywhere. Even if one becomes afraid and starts running one is not able to break free or to escape. Thus one has the suffering of limitless fear and dread.

The bardo of becoming is like being a feather carried in the wind without any power over where it is taken. One has come from somewhere but has no idea what is coming next. One does not know one's final destination. One cannot remain at the point where this bardo commenced but must go weeping wherever one is taken. With an unhappy heart one sobs with grief. Day and night cannot be distinguished and one encounters neither familiar places nor people. It is as if one is being drawn towards a quite unknown land.

In the bardo of becoming, mind and body start a new experience since one cannot retreat as one lacks the power to re-enter the elements and skandhas of one's previous life. Perhaps one's corpse was burnt without trace, or put in the ground or eaten by birds, anyway it is impossible to find. No matter where one goes one cannot find it. Nor can one rest in one spot. Abject and sobbing one shudders in desolate terror. The breath that one rode like a horse has lost its former body and wanders here and there without any sense of direction as if being harried by wild animals. There are mountains in avalanche, flooding oceans, great infernos, impenetrable black rainfall and one is driven by ferocious winds. Hunted by soldiers, there are howling sounds and the noise of beating and killing. Terrified of all this, one flees anywhere one can. Yet though one flees one finds no relief for there is no protection. Without being able to choose, one must take birth in one of the six realms. One goes searching and running but due to one's previously created karma one must wander in limbo before one's next life.

An example to show the basis of all the bardos: a person who is in charge of looking after his dwelling has strayed. He wants to return to his own place but he doesn't know where it is and must travel on without knowing where he is.

These are the examples for the bardos.

Vajra Vows

EIGHTH, THE SIGNS OF THE BARDOS

In *the bardo of birth* one has an illusory body. There the material form of flesh, blood, skandhas and dhātus has a precise existence which seems substantial, yet it is like a reflection seen in water or in a mirror. It casts no shadow in the light of the sun or the moon. This forms the basis for the development of the flesh and blood body.

The sign of the bardo of dreams is that insubstantial confusing appearances arise in many different forms.

The signs of the bardo of death consists of the six kinds of indication: outer, inner, secret, distant, proximate and partial.

Firstly make food offerings to the Guru, Deva and Dakini and with the support of the torma (gTor-Ma) symbolic cake, for the protectors, invite them for the serkyem[6] offering and then offer the benefits arising from this to all beings.

FIRST INDICATION, *the outer signs by which one can see if one is about to die or not*

One's body feels heavy, one loses one's appetite and the senses become dull. One gets angry and the mind is gradually permeated by sorrow. One has turbulent dreams and the colour of one's body changes frequently. The colour goes from one's nails. When these things happen one has nine months or half a day to live. When pus comes from one's eyes one will die in five months. When the hair at the back of one's head points up one will die in three months. When one urinates on sneezing, when urine, excrement and semen come out at the same time, when the colour of one's face changes during different activities, when one's senses are sometimes clear and sometimes unclear, when one's eyebrows grow further apart, when perspiration steams from one's head. These are all signs that one has gone into the hand of Yama, the lord of death.

When one closes both eyes with one's index fingers and sees swirling light but not in the left eye then one will die in six months. If there is no movement in the right eye then one will be dead in ten days. If the index fingers are put in one's earholes and no sound enters then one has been bound in the ropes of Yama.

If one was angry in former times but is much more angry now, if one does not keep one's promises and is afraid of where one stays, if one has little faith in one's heart for the Dharma, if one is angry with holy people and feels sorrow wherever one stays. These indications of death are the outer signs.

SECOND INDICATION, *the inner signs are those concerning dreams and breath*

At dawn of the first day of the first month of the Tibetan calendar sit up straight. If the air comes from the left nostril for three days followed by three days from the right then that balance means it is not time for one to die. If the order is reversed then one will certainly die soon. If breath comes from both nostrils at the same time then one will die in three days. If both nostrils are blocked and breath comes in through the mouth then one will die immediately.

If the following dreams occur before or just after midnight then they carry no fixed significance. If they occur in the two hours before dawn then their consequence is certain.

To dream of a cat riding a white monkey and coming from the east, or of tigers, foxes, corpses, buffalos, pigs, apes, insects coming in a crowd from the south. These are signs of death and so one must do practice to repulse death.

THIRD INDICATION, *the secret signs of death*

If on the morning of the first day of the year, black semen and white sweat emerge, it is said that this is a sign one will die in two months. If the semen is red one will die in six months. If the semen is white and hot one will not immediately decline. If one is breathing through one's nostrils one will not die as life is protected. If one's semen is frequently discharged one will die in four months. If a new black mole develops near the urethra and one has many desires these are signs of death and one must practise a ransoming ritual meditation.

FOURTH INDICATION, *the distant signs of death*

In an isolated place look at the sky on the first day of the first month of the year in the morning or afternoon, or else in the evening of the fifteenth day, or at twilight and in the pre-dawn period. In these calm periods when the sky is clear, sit naked and pray very strongly. Recite this king of mantras one hundred times: "OM AE YE SHE PA RA HA KA RA TE SHA RE HUNG PHAT!" Recite the names of the Buddhas of the ten directions. Request them to hold back the sun and the moon and write a letter A in one's shadow at the location of one's heart. Keep one's eyes focused on it, very straight and steady, and stabilise one's mind. If one's eyes start moving look into the sky. One's own reflection will arise in the sky as a sign. If it is broken or unclear that is a sign of certain imminent death. If the sky's colour is not clear do the mantra practice again and again. If the sky is a pure white colour that is the sign of a long life.

FIFTH INDICATION, *the signs of proximate death*

One's teeth become covered with a strong black dirt. This is called the arrival of the demonic form of one's own elements, and one will die within nine days. When the nostrils collapse blocking the flow of air, if one's arms start waving in and out, this is called the demon Rila Nyagpa and indicates death in five days. If the eyes develop a fixed stare then death will come within three days. If one can see one's nose directly then one will be dead in seven days. If tears cease in one's eyes one will die in five days. If black semen comes on one's tongue, developing gradually, then one will be dead within two days. If the diaphragm collapses and the nostrils too then this is a sign of imminent death.

More particularly, this is the method for understanding the signs of death. At midday face south, sit and put your right elbow on your raised right knee. Put your palm at your forehead so that your wrist is in front of your eyes. Look at it and it will become narrower. If it shrinks so that it looks as if it were split by a shadow then you will die in nineteen days. These are the ways of identifying the proximate signs of death.

SIXTH INDICATION, *the partial signs of death*

If one's eyes cannot see one's nose then death comes in five months. If one cannot see the tip of one's tongue then one will die in three days. If one cannot see one's left side reflected in a mirror then that is a sign that one will die in seven months. If one feels heat when one breathes on the palm of one's hand that is a sign of death. If one's reflection in water is only half there that is a sign of death. If sweat does not remain on the chest and if sweat does not dry, and if a person has lice eggs – these are signs of death.

Signs that death is near

The outer signs are that food and drink are vomited and the body has little warmth. The head droops, the complexion becomes lifeless and the senses are dulled. The five elements within sink into the flesh and bones. This is a sign that the outer elements are sinking into the earth. The body becomes heavy, has no heat and seems to fall below the earth. Earth merges into water and there is a loss of form. The body loses its power and the mind becomes dull.

The signs of blood and lymph merging into water are that fluid appears in the mouth and nose, the tongue becomes dry, and the diaphragm collapses. As water sinks into fire the body loses its heat. The mind fluctuates between clarity and loss of clarity.

The signs that the inner heat has merged into the fire element are that the body loses all its heat, the eyes turn up and others are no longer recognised.

When fire merges with wind all sense of light vanishes. The breath in the body merges into the air element and the sign of this is panting. Consciousness sinks as if a mirage were occurring. Lice and their eggs all leave the body.

The blood that one got from one's mother and that has remained below the navel rises up and one experiences red images. At that time the appearances that stem from desire and the forty kinds of thoughts that desire engenders all cease.

The white semen that one got from one's father and which has remained at the top of one's head descends and due to this white and yellow images occur. All the thirty-three kinds of thoughts that arise from anger cease.

The breath comes in gulps each one getting longer and longer.

All the blood enters the life channel and then gathers in the heart as a ball of blood which gives rise to the experience of black darkness. It is as dark as if one were in a house that had fallen down.

At that time all the experiences one has are due to stupidity and then the seventy kinds of thoughts arising from stupidity all cease.

The mouth is open, the eyes look up and are blank. Outer appearances are like the setting sun. The doors of the senses close and all appearances become dark and then all images and memories cease. The breath stretches no further than an elbow span. Inner experience is like a dark night.

Then in the centre of the heart the blood and semen come together. The head slumps and the breath extends to a full arm span.

Then in the heart the three balls of blood and semen meet causing the breath to pant and to extend for a full double arm span. It is very dark, there is no memory and the outer breath ceases.

The ascending blood and the descending semen meet in the heart. In the consequent situation of happiness, consciousness vanishes. Consciousness merges into natural clarity and due to this there is the experience of union, of co-emergent bliss and original knowing.

In the heart awareness experiences the meeting of mother and son actualities. The inner breath is finished and wind and mind enter the central channel. Then the ground natural clarity arises for all sentient beings.

For a yogi who has meditation experience and the clarity arising from the path, the mother and son instantly meet. One ascends directly to the unborn Dharmakāya with Sambhogakāya and Nirmanakāya manifesting effortlessly for the benefit of beings. With these three modes of enlightenment effortlessly arising, Buddhahood is manifest.

Ignorant beings who have not meditated experience the arising of the clarity of actuality, but do not recognise it. Due to this they are reborn again and again, countless times.

Although the dawning of the ground natural clarity is inexpressible, recognition of it frees one from the obscurations of the torpor of co-emergent ignorance. Otherwise one wanders without limit in limitless samsara.

For this reason now that one has obtained a human body it is very important to practise the profound meditation instructions. Obtain instructions from a good teacher or from vow-keeping friends and practise the phowa meditation to transfer one's consciousness out of one's body.

The signs of the bardo of actuality are that the appearance of sounds, lights and rays will occur. The sign of sounds is that if one puts one's index fingers in one's ears one hears a roaring sound[7]. When one is in the bardo of actuality one hears a sound like the roaring of a thousand dragons. The sign of light is that if one puts one's index fingers in one's eyes, one sees lights. When one is in the bardo it is full of colours and the bodies of the peaceful and wrathful deities. The sign of rays is that when one looks at the light of the sun and moon the light rays arise as a sequence of spheres of light. This is the sign of what actually arises as light rays in the bardo.

The signs of the bardo of becoming are that when one emerges from profound unconscious sleep[8] many different dreams appear. In this bardo the mental body one has can pass unobstructed through mountains and rocks. This body casts no shadow nor does it leave any footprint or make any reflection. This is a sign that it is free of the elements and skandhas.

Thus is the explanation of the signs of the six bardos.

Vajra Vows

Translated by C.R. Lama and James Low in 1979
Revised by James Low in 2013

Notes

¹ Vajra Vows reminds the Guardians of this text that it is carefully protected and sealed so that its authentic meaning will not be tampered with.

² Although the text says 'eighteen' only thirteen are listed and this translation covers only eight.

³ The eighteen elements of experience: the six sense organs (with the heart for the mind); the six senses (including the mind); the six sense objects (including thoughts and feelings).

⁴ The sense objects and consciousnesses.

⁵ The five heaps which constitute a person: form, feeling, perceptual organisation, association, consciousness.

⁶ The gSer-sKyems offering of tea or alcohol is made in order to propitiate and encourage the dharma protectors.

⁷ This sound is taken to indicate the self-existing sound intrinsic to the open space of being.

⁸ This sleep is not the ordinary sleep of night-time but is the deep blank unconsciousness which can occur at the end of the bardo of actuality when, due to not recognising the nature of the wrathful forms that appear, one falls unconscious from terror.

4

ༀྃ༔ བར་དོའི་རྩ་ཚིག་བཞུགས་སོ༔

The Root Verses
of
the Bardos

རྒྱལ་བ་ཞི་ཁྲོའི་སྤྲ་ལ་ཕྱག་འཚལ་ལོ༔ བར་དོ་རྣམ་པ་དྲུག་གི་རྩ་ཚིག་ནི༔

Salutation to the peaceful and wrathful jinas. This is a summary of the six bardos.

ཀྱེ་མ་བདག་ལ་སྐྱེ་གནས་བར་དོ་འཆར་དུས་འདིར༔

KYE MA		DAG	LA	KYE NAE	BAR DO	CHAR	DU	DIR
alas! (how sad to be trapped in ignorance)		*me*	*to, for*	*birthplace*	*intermediate (i.e. life time from birth or the moment of conception until death)*	*arising*	*time*	*here**

* *i.e. when it happens to me*

Alas! Now when the bardo of life is arising for me,

ཚེ་ལ་ལོང་མེད་ལེ་ལོ་སྤང་བྱས་ནས༔

TSHE	LA	LONG	ME	LE LO	PANG	JAE	NE
life	*in*	*leisure*	*without*	*laziness*	*abandon, stop*	*do*	*then*
(i.e. life is very short, and we do not know when it will end)							

I must abandon all laziness during my span which is too short for leisure.

ཐོས་བསམ་སྒོམ་གསུམ་མ་ཡེངས་ལམ་དུ་འཆུག༔

THO	SAM	GOM	SUM	MA YENG	LAM	DU	JUG
hearing, studying	reflecting	meditating	three	unwavering, undistracted	path	in, on	enter, keep to

Keeping to the path of undistracted listening, reflecting and meditating,

སྣང་སེམས་ལམ་སློང་སྐུ་གསུམ་མངོན་འགྱུར་སྦྱངས༔

NANG	SEM	LAM	LONG	KU	SUM	NGON GYUR	JANG
appearances, ideas *	mind, citta	path	go well	modes	three #	become manifest, develop clearly	practise

* seeing both in sunyata   # Dharmakaya, Sambhogakaya, Nirmanakaya

I must progress on the path of understanding the nature of appearances and mind, and practise making the three modes of enlightenment manifest.

མི་ལུས་ལན་གཅིག་ཐོབ་པའི་དུས་ཚོད་འདིར༔

MI	LU	LAN	CHIG	THOB PAI	DU TSHOD	DIR
human	body	time	one	get	time	here

(To gain a human birth, especially one with the 18 freedoms and opportunities, uses up so much good karma that it is very difficult to get one again.)

Now at this time when I have gained my sole chance of a human birth

ཡེངས་པ་ལམ་ལ་སྟོང་པའི་དུས་མ་ཡིན༔

YENG PA	LAM	LA	TONG PAI	DU	MA	YIN
vacillating, uncertain, hazy	path	to, on	leisure	time	not	have

I have no time to waste on the path of vacillation.

Alas. Now when the bardo of life is arising for me I must abandon all laziness during my span which is too short for leisure. Keeping to the path of undistracted listening, reflecting and meditating, I must progress on the path of understanding the nature of appearances and mind, and practise making the three modes of enlightenment manifest. Now at this time when I have gained my sole chance of a human birth, I have no time to waste on the path of vacillation.

(Alternative reading)

[Note: There is also a tradition of the six lines of these verses being read in the line order 1, 5, 6, 2, 3, 4 as below.]

Alas! Now when the bardo of life is arising for me, now at this time when I have gained my sole chance of a human birth, I have no time to waste on the path of vacillation. I must abandon all laziness during my span which is too short for leisure, and keeping to the path of undistracted listening,

*reflecting and meditating, I must progress on the path of understanding
the nature of appearances and mind, and practise making the three modes
of enlightenment manifest.*

ཀྱེ་མ་བདག་ལ་རྨི་ལམ་བར་དོ་འཆར་དུས་འདིར༔

KYE MA	DAG LA	MI LAM	BAR DO	CHAR	DU	DIR
las!	*me to*	*dream*	*intermediate period*	*arising*	*time*	*here, now (i.e. when it happens for me)*

Alas! Now when the bardo of dreams is arising for me,

གཏི་མུག་རོ་ཉལ་བག་མེད་སྤང་བྱས་ནས༔

TI MUG	RO NYAL	BAG ME	PANG	JAE	NE
stupidity, mental dullness	*sleeping like a corpse*	*careless, unheeding*	*abandon*	*do*	*then*

I must abandon the unheeding, corpse-like sleep of stupidity and

དྲན་པ་ཡེངས་མེད་གནས་ལུགས་ངང་ལ་འཇོག༔

DRAN PA	YENG ME	NAE LUG	NGANG	LA	JOG
attention, recollection of awareness	*unwavering*	*natural mode, original condition*	*openness*	*in*	*enter and keep*

Keep to the openness of my original situation with unwavering recollection.

རྨི་ལམ་བཟུང་ལ་སྤྲུལ་བསྒྱུར་འོད་གསལ་སྦྱང༔

MI LAM	ZUNG	LA	TRUL GYUR	OD SAL	JANG
dream (be aware of it and its nature and not forget it upon awakening)	*hold*	*with, thus*	*transform it with the understanding of its illusoriness*	*clear illumination, natural clarity, self-luminous quality*	*practice*

Being aware of my dreams as they come, I must transform them into the
practice of natural radiance.

དུད་འགྲོ་བཞིན་དུ་ཉལ་བར་མི་བྱ་བར༔

DUD DRO	ZHIN DU	NYAL WAR	MI	JA WAR
animal (i.e. with a dull mind)	*as*	*sleep*	*not*	*doing*

Not sleeping like an animal

གཉིད་དང་མངོན་སུམ་འདྲེས་པའི་ཉམས་ལེན་གཅེས༔

NYI	DANG	NGON SUM	DRE PAI	NYAM LEN	CHE
sleep	*and*	*direct knowledge*	*mix, merge*	*practice*	*very important, precious*

I will follow this very important practice of merging sleep with the direct
experience of my true nature.

Alas! Now when the bardo of dreams is arising for me, I must abandon the unheeding corpse-like sleep of stupidity and keep to the openness of my original situation with unwavering recollection. Being aware of my dreams as they come, I must transform them into the practice of clear radiance. Not sleeping like an animal I will follow this very important practice of merging sleep with the direct experience my true nature.

(Alternative reading)

Alas! Now when the bardo of dreams is arising for me, without sleeping like an animal I will follow this very important practice of merging sleep with the direct experience of my true nature. I must abandon the unheeding corpse-like sleep of stupidity and keep to the openness of my original situation with unwavering recollection. Being aware of my dreams as they come, I must transform them into the practice of clear radiance.

ཀྱེ་མ་བདག་ལ་བསམ་གཏན་བར་དོ་འཆར་དུས་འདིར༔

KYE MA	DAG LA	SAM TAN	BAR DO	CHAR	DU	DIR
alas!	*me to*	*mental stability, meditation*	*intermediate period*	*arising*	*time*	*here, now (i.e. when it happens for me)*

Alas! Now when the bardo of mental stability is arising for me,

རྣམ་ཡེངས་འཁྲུལ་བའི་ཚོགས་རྣམས་སྤངས་བྱས་ནས༔

NAM YENG	TRUL WAI	TSHOG NAM	PANG JAE	NE
very wavering	*confusion*	*many different kinds*	*abandon*	*then*
(i.e. all the thoughts that arise from uncertainty about the true nature)				

I must abandon all the different forms of vacillating confusion and

ཡེངས་མེད་འཛིན་མེད་མཐའ་བྲལ་ངང་དུ་འཇུག༔

YENG ME	DZIN ME	THA DRAL	NGANG DU	JUG
unwavering (always in mNyam-bZhag, meditation)	*without grasping (always in rJe-Thob, post-meditation)*	*free of all limits, no reifying conceptualisation*	*openness in*	*keep, enter and stay*

Keep to the unwavering, ungrasping openness free of all limits.

བསྐྱེད་རྫོགས་གཉིས་ལ་བརྟན་པ་ཐོབ་པར་བྱ༔

KYED	DZOG	NYI	LA	TAN PA	TOB PA	JA
developing system	*perfecting system*	*two*	*to, in*	*stability*	*get, keep*	*do*

I must gain stability in both the developing and perfecting systems.

བྱ་བ་སྤངས་ནས་རྩེ་གཅིག་སྒྲུབ་དུས་འདིར༔

JA WA	PANG	NE	TSE CHIG	DRUB	DU	DIR
activity (dualistic and worldly)	abandon	then	one-pointedly	practise	time	here, now

Abandoning all worldly activities I will practise one-pointedly here and now.

ཉོན་མོངས་འཁྲུལ་པའི་དབང་དུ་མ་བཏང་ཞིག༔

NYON MONG	TRUL PAI	WANG	DU	MA	TANG	ZHIG
afflictions (anger, desire, etc.)	confusion	power	under	not	go, send myself	must

I must not go under the bewildering power of the afflictions.

Alas! Now when the bardo of mental stability is arising for me, I must abandon all the different forms of vacillating confusion and keep to the unwavering, ungrasping openness free of all limits. I must gain stability in both the developing and perfecting systems. Abandoning all worldly activities, I will practise one-pointedly here and now. I must not go under the bewildering power of the afflictions.

(Alternative reading)

Alas! Now when the bardo of mental stability is arising for me, I will abandon all worldly activity and practise one-pointedly here and now. I must not go under the bewildering power of the afflictions. I must abandon all the different forms of vacillating confusion and keep to the unwavering, ungrasping openness free of all limits. I must gain stability in both the developing and perfecting systems.

ཀྱེ་མ་བདག་ལ་འཆི་ཁ་བར་དོ་འཆར་དུས་འདིར༔

KYE MA	DAG	LA	CHI KHA	BAR DO	CHAR	DU	DIR
alas!	me	to	death time	period	arising	time	here, now (i.e. when it happens for me)

Alas! Now when the bardo of dying is arising for me,

ཀུན་ལ་ཆགས་སེམས་ཞེན་འཛིན་སྤངས་བྱས་ལ༔

KUN	LA	CHAG SEM	ZHEN	DZIN	PANG	JAE	LA
all (worldly things)	to	desireful mind	hopes, expectations	grasping	abandon	do	then

I must abandon all hopes, desires and grasping.

གདམས་ངག་གསལ་བའི་ལམ་ལ་མ་ཡེངས་འཇུག༔

DAM NGAG	SAL WAI	LAM	LA	MA YENG	JUG
instructions, doctrines	clear (i.e. keeping them clearly in mind)	path	on	unwavering	enter, keep

Keeping unwaveringly on the clear path of the dharma instructions,

རང་རིག་སྐྱེ་མེད་ནམ་མཁའི་དབྱིངས་སུ་འཕོ༔

RANG RIG	KYE ME	NAM KHAI	YING	SU	PHO
own awareness, mind	unborn	sky's (sunyata)	depth	in	send, merge (like a bubble rising in boiling water)

I must integrate my awareness in the unborn sky-like space.

འདུས་བྱས་ཤ་ཁྲག་ལུས་དང་བྲལ་ལ་ཁད༔

DU JAE	SHA	TRAG	LU	DANG	DRAL	LA KHAD
compounded	flesh	blood	body		free of	almost to, almost, on the point of

Now, as I am becoming free of this compounded body of flesh and blood,

མི་རྟག་སྒྱུ་མ་ཡིན་པར་ཤེས་པར་བྱ༔

MI TAG	GYU MA	YIN PAR	SHE PAR	JA
impermanent	illusory	is as	know	do

I must know it to be impermanent and illusory.

Alas! Now when the bardo of dying is arising for me, I must abandon all hopes, desires, and grasping. Keeping unwaveringly on the clear path of the dharma instructions, I must integrate my awareness in the unborn sky-like space. Now, as I am becoming free of this compounded body of flesh and blood, I must know it to be impermanent and illusory.

(Alternative reading)

Alas! Now when the bardo of dying is arising for me, now as I am becoming free of this compounded body of flesh and blood, I must know it to be impermanent and illusory. I must abandon all hopes, desires, and grasping and keep unwaveringly to the clear path of the dharma instructions. I must integrate my awareness in the unborn sky-like space.

ཀྱེ་མ་བདག་ལ་ཆོས་ཉིད་བར་དོ་འཆར་དུ་འདིར༔

KYE MA	DAG	LA	CHO NYID	BAR DO	CHAR	DU	DIR
alas!	me	to	dharmata, actuality original situation	period	arising (it starts to appear just after death)	time	here

Alas! Now when the bardo of actuality is arising for me,

ཀུན་ལ་དངངས་སྐྲག་འཇིགས་ནང་སྤང་སྤངས་བྱས་ནས༔

KUN	LA	NGANG	TRAG	JIG	NANG	PANG JAE	NE
all (that appears)	to	fear	fear	terror	ideas	abandon	then

I must abandon all fearful and terrified notions about all that is occurring, and

གང་ཤར་རང་སྣང་རིག་པར་ངོ་ཤེས་བྱ༔

GANG	SHAR	RANG NANG	RIG PAR	NGO SHE	JA
whatever	arises	own idea	awareness, as	recognise	do

Recognise that whatever arises is the natural radiance of my own awareness.

བར་དོའི་སྣང་ཚུལ་ཡིན་པར་ཤེས་པར་བྱ༔

BAR DOI	NANG TSHUL	YIN PAR	SHE PAR	JA
bardo's	form of arising	is, as	know	do

I must know that this is the mode of appearance of this bardo.

དོན་ཆེན་འགག་གས་ལ་ཐུགས་པའི་དུས་གཅིག་འོང༔

DON CHEN	GAG	LA	THUG PAI	DU	CHIG	ONG
great meaning, the important point	stop	to	impatient *(i.e. very pressing and urgent and necessary to use)*	time	one	come

Now when this very important and crucial time is coming

རང་སྣང་ཞི་ཁྲོའི་ཚོགས་ལ་མ་འཇིགས་ཞིག༔

RANG NANG	ZHI	TROI	TSHOG LA	MA JIG	ZHIG
own ideas, my own notions	peaceful	wrathful	hosts to	not afraid	must be

I must not be afraid of the hosts of peaceful and wrathful forms that are my own luminosity.

Alas! Now when the bardo of the actuality is arising for me, I must abandon all fearful and terrified notions about whatever occurs, and recognise that whatever arises is the natural radiance of my own awareness. I must know that this is the mode of appearance of this bardo. Now when this very important and crucial time is coming I must not be afraid of the hosts of peaceful and wrathful forms that are my own luminosity.

(Alternative reading)

Alas! Now when the bardo of actuality is arising for me, now when this very important and crucial time is coming, I must not be afraid of the hosts of peaceful and wrathful forms that are my own luminosity. I must abandon all fearful and terrified notions about all that is occurring and recognise that whatever arises is the natural radiance of my own awareness. I must know that this is the mode of appearance of this bardo.

ཀྱི་མ་བདག་ལ་སྲིད་པ་བར་དོ་འཆར་དུས་འདིརཿ

KYE MA	DAG	LA	SID PA	BAR DO	CHAR	DU	DIR
alas!	*me*	*to*	*possible worldly existence, rebirth*	*period*	*arising*	*time*	*now (i.e. when this is happening to me)*

Alas! Now when the bardo of rebirth is arising for me,

འདུན་པ་རྩེ་གཅིག་སེམས་ལ་བཟུང་བྱས་ནསཿ

DUN PA	TSE CHIG	SEM	LA	ZUNG JAE	NE
devotion, longing	*one-pointed*	*mind*	*in, as*	*hold*	*then*

(keeping one-pointedly on pure dharma thoughts and the understanding of non-duality)

I must keep my mind in one-pointed devotion and

བཟང་པོ་ལས་ཀྱི་འཕྲོ་ལ་ནན་གྱིས་འཐུདཿ

ZANG PO	LAE	KYI	TRO	LA	NAN GYI	THUD
good	*karma*	*of*	*arising*	*to*	*urgent, pressing*	*extend, assist encourage*

(This is the moment to strive for a good rebirth and for that, much good karma is necessary, so we must make only good thoughts arise.)

Strongly encourage the maturing of my good karma.

མངལ་སྒོ་དགགས་ནས་རུ་ལོག་དྲན་པར་བྱཿ

NGAL	GO	GAG	NE	RU LOG	DRAN PAR	JA
womb	*door*	*stop, close*	*then*	*reverse*	*remember*	*do*

(the entrance into the six realms)

(go back through the stages of dependent origination, right up to ignorance[1], and then transcend it)

Closing the womb door I must remember to reverse the process that leads to existence.

སྙིང་རུས་དག་སྣང་དགོས་པའི་དུས་གཅིག་ཡིནཿ

NYING RU	DAG NANG	GO PAI	DU	CHIG	YIN
strong, genuine	*faith, pure view*	*need*	*time*	*one*	*is*

This is the one time when authentic pure vision is required, so

མིག་སེར་སྤངས་ནས་བླ་མ་ཡབ་ཡུམ་སྒོམཿ

MIG SER	PANG	NE	LA MA	YAB YUM	GOM
jealousy	*abandon*	*then*	*guru*	*with his consort*	*meditate on this*

(As one approaches and is about to be born into the womb of a woman making love one very strongly meditates that the couple is in fact one's guru with his or her consort and in this way all desireful attachments are destroyed and the impulse to enter will be overcome. If we do enter, it will be by merging with their nectar.)

Abandoning all jealousy, I will meditate on my guru with his consort.

Alas! Now when the bardo of rebirth is arising for me, I must keep my mind in one-pointed devotion and strongly encourage the maturing of my good karma. Closing the womb door I must remember to reverse the process that leads to existence. This is the one time when authentic pure vision is required so, abandoning all jealousy, I will meditate on my guru with his consort.

(Alternative reading)

Alas! Now when the bardo of rebirth is arising for me, this is the one time when authentic pure vision is required so, abandoning all jealousy, I will meditate on my guru with his consort. I must keep my mind in one-pointed devotion and strongly encourage the maturing of my good karma. Closing the womb door I must remember to reverse the process that leads to existence.

འཆི་བ་འོང་སྙམ་མེད་པའི་བློ་རིང་པོ༔

CHI WA	ONG	NYAM MED PAI	LO RING PO
death	coming	unthoughtful, of	unbelieving

Thoughtlessly never believing that death will come

དོན་མེད་ཚེ་འདིའི་བྱ་བ་བསྒྲུབས་བསྒྲུབས་ནས༔

DON ME	TSHE	DI	JA WA	DRUB DRUB	NE
meaningless, worthless (i.e. actions that do not lead to awakening)	life	this	deeds, activities	done done (i.e. very much, all the time)	then

I have passed this life in the constant practice of meaningless activity,

ད་རེས་སྟོང་ལོག་བྱ་ན་འདུན་མ་འཁྲུལ༔

DA RE	TONG LOG	JA	NA	DUN MA TRUL
now	empty-handed, without anything useful	act like that	if	failure and loss

And now if I go from it empty-handed, that will be a great loss and failure.

དགོས་ངེས་ཤེས་པ་དམ་པའི་ཆོས་ཡིན་པས༔

GOE	NGE	SHE PA	DAM PAI	CHO YIN PAE
necessary	certain	understanding	holy, excellent (for it alone can help at the time of death)	dharma is, therefore

I must remember that the one certain necessity is the holy dharma.

ད་ལྟ་ཉིད་དུ་ལྷ་ཆོས་མི་བྱེད་དམ༔

DAN TA NYID DU	LHA CHO	MI JED	DAM
now, immediately	meditation on the gods	not do	or

Therefore if now, at this moment, I do not meditate on the divine forms or

དྲིན་ཅན་བླ་མའི་ཞལ་ནས་འདི་སྐད་གསུངས༔

DRIN CHEN	**LA MAI**	**ZHAL**	**NE**	**DI**	**KAD**	**SUNG**
kind	*guru's*	*mouth*	*from*	*these*	*words*	*spoken*

Bear in mind the instructions that I have received

བླ་མའི་གདམས་ངག་སེམས་ལ་མ་བཞག་ན༔

LA MAI	**DAM NGAG**	**SEM**	**LA**	**MA**	**ZHAG**	**NA**
guru's	*instructions*	*mind*	*in*	*not*	*put*	*if*

From my very kind guru's own mouth,

རང་གིས་རང་ཉིད་བསླུས་པར་མི་འགྱུར་རམ༔

RANG	**GI**	**RANG NYID**	**LU PAR**	**MI**	**GYUR**	**RAM**
self	*by*	*self*	*deceived, cheated*	*not*	*become*	*or*

Will I not be my own deceiver?

Thoughtlessly never believing that death will come I have passed this life in the constant practice of meaningless activity, and now if I go from it empty-handed, that will be a great loss and failure. I must remember that the one certain necessity is the holy dharma. Therefore if now, at this moment, I do not meditate on the divine forms or bear in mind the instructions that I have received from my very kind guru's own mouth, will I not be my own deceiver?

བར་དོ་རྣམ་པ་དྲུག་གི་རྩ་ཚིག་རྫོགས་སོ༔

This concludes *The Root Verses of the Six Bardos*, from the terma of Karma Lingpa.

Translated by C.R. Lama and James Low at Santiniketan, Bengal, India 1978

Revised by James Low, June 2013

Notes

[1] Refer to Page 11 of Chapter 1, the section entitled 'Cutting through, or Indirect Experience'.

5

Vajrasattva Meditation Purifying All Errors and Obscurations

The Text

There are six aspects to this subject:

1. The *ground* on which errors are purified.
2. The *errors* which are to be purified.
3. The *method* by which the errors are purified.
4. The *results* gained by purifying errors.
5. The *difficulties* experienced when errors are not purified.
6. The *benefits* of expiating errors.

1. The Ground or Basis on which Errors are Purified

The original ground (*gZhi*) nature of enlightenment, primordial buddhahood, has always been present within the minds of all sentient beings. Just as the clear sky can be covered by clouds which appear suddenly, so that original nature can seem to be contaminated by manifold faulty dualistic notions. But just as the original nature of the sky itself is free from even the least fault or good quality [such as clouds or sunshine], so the natural presence of mind is pure in itself for the obscurations, false ideas and afflictions are merely adventitious.

So if we ask what is the manner of existence of the ground, its nature is absolutely pure in the same way that a piece of coal whose nature is black never becomes white.

2. The Errors which are to be Purified

All sentient beings, all who exist in the six realms of the desire, form and formless dimensions are caught in the net of thoughts or defilements arising from the suddenly occurring belief in duality. In all their lives during beginningless time up until now, they have developed the obscurations of karma arising from the ten unvirtuous actions, the five unlimited errors, the five similar errors, four heavy errors, the eight wrong practices[1] and all that is naturally wrong.

For example, just as verdigris can arise from the surface of a copper mirror, so the subtle traces of the obscurations of that which can be known abide on the actual nature of the ground of all.

"TIME, INVOLVEMENT, THOUGHT, OBJECT, NATURE AND MEANS OF ARISING ARE THE SIX WAYS BY WHICH KARMA IS ACCUMULATED."

   i. *TIME:* during all our lifetimes in beginningless samsara up until now, many errors have been accumulated.

  ii. *INVOLVEMENT:* errors and unvirtuous activity have been committed by oneself, and one has encouraged others to do such things and one has been pleased by these bad actions committed by others.

 iii. *THOUGHT:* the varied thoughts arising from the five poisonous afflictions of assumption, attraction, aversion, pride and jealousy develop the many errors which are accumulated.

  iv. *OBJECT:* errors are accumulated on the basis of one's connection with those excellent objects, the guru and the three jewels – buddha, dharma and sangha – and with one's parents.

   v. *NATURE:* there are doctrinally defined lapses, naturally defined lapses and conventional lapses.

  vi. *MEANS OF ARISING:* the errors and obscurations arise via one's body, voice and mind.

3. The Method by which Errors are Purified

There are four aspects to this:

    a. The potency of the field of activity.

    b. The potency of effective application of antidotes.

    c. The potency of total renunciation.

    d. The potency of abandoning the return to error.

a. *The potency of the field of activity*

I imagine that in front of me are all my enemies and those who are angry with me. On my right side is my father and on my left side is my mother. At my back are troublesome demons. We are surrounded by all sentient beings, as many as would fill the sky.

In the sky just in front of the crown of my head, resting on cushions of lotus, sun and moon is the glorious lord Vajrasattva who encompasses the nature of all the buddhas of the three times. He is white in colour, blazing with infinite light and splendour, like a snow mountain in the light of a million suns. He has one face and two hands. The right hand holds a vajra which symbolises the unchanging nature of awareness and emptiness. His left hand holds against his thigh a silver bell which symbolises the union of appearance and emptiness. He sits with his left foot tucked in and his right foot slightly extended, in the posture of a Bodhisattva. He displays the nine peaceful aspects. These are that he is soft, pliable, capable of all possible movements, fluid, youthful looking, transparent, shining, relaxed and impressive. His body is beautifully adorned with the thirteen ornaments of the sambhogakaya. These are the crown of the five buddha families, earrings, short necklace, medium necklace to the level of the heart, long necklace to the navel, bracelets, anklets, jeweled belt, upper white silk bodice, multi-coloured silk dhoti, yellow scarf/sash, multi-coloured ribbon under the crown and long scarf draped over the shoulders.

In the centre of his heart upon a moon disc is the white seed letter Hung (ཧཱུྃ) which is the essence of his being. Around it, like a necklace of pearls, revolves the hundred-syllable mantra. Revolving to the right, the mantra emits countless rays of light which rise up as offerings to the pure realms and also descend to remove all the suffering in the six realms. Thus one benefits both oneself and others.

The rays of light gather back together within Vajrasattva and then a flow of liberating elixir descends and emerges from the big toe of his right foot. Entering through the crowns of the heads of myself and of all sentient beings, it gradually fills our bodies. All the wrong deeds, obscurations and subtle karmic traces that we have accumulated since beginningless time appear as liquid coal dust and sooty water, and all sicknesses appear in the form of blood and pus. All demons and impure forces appear in the form of snakes and insects, scorpions, tadpoles and so forth.

All our obscurations and impurities appear as smoke and steam and exit from our anuses and descend without resting on any of the nine realms below the earth's surface. Then they enter the open mouth of the lord of death, *Las-Kyi gShin-rJe,* who has been appointed to this duty by all the buddhas of the three times. They also enter the mouths of all demons and trouble makers and by this they become happy and satisfied. All our outstanding debts are paid off and all troublesome claimants are satisfied. Untimely death, difficulties and obstacles – all these are removed for myself and all sentient beings. All our hopes and wishes are fulfilled. We should believe that all karma and obscurations of the lords of death, all sicknesses and diseases, and all troublemakers are purified.

In this way we are cleansed and purified by the stream of liberating elixir. Remaining in this situation, one should avoid frivolous socialising and distractions, cease ordinary conversation and focus one-pointedly on recitation of the hundred-syllable mantra:

Om Vajrasattva Samayam Anupalaya Vajrasattva Tvenopatistha Dridho Me Bhava Sutosyo Me Bhava Suposyo Me Bhava Anurakto Me Bhava Sarva Siddhim Me Prayaccha Sarva Karma Suca Me Cittam Sreyam Kuru Hum Ha Ha Ha Ha Ho Bhagavan Sarva Tathagata Vajra Ma Me Munca Vajri Bhava Mahasamayasattva Aa

We can also use the letters of the mantra as a way of briefly expressing how the ground arises on the ground itself; that is, the understanding of the original knowing of the expanse of the original ground:

OM indicates the ground original situation of the inseparability of modality (*sKu*) and original knowing (*Ye-Shes*).

VAJRASATTVA SAMAYAM indicates that the ground original situation of inseparability is Vajrasattva's primordial commitment to the nature of all samsara and nirvana.

ANUPALAYA indicates that I will truly hold to awakening in the naturally occurring great enlightenment of the primordial actuality which is the true nature of Vajrasattva who abides as the original actual nature.

VAJRASATTVA TVENOPATISTHA indicates that with this authentic experience one should not search far and wide for Vajrasattva since from the very beginning one has always remained with him, without any actual separation.

DRIDHO ME BHAVA What is called 'I' or 'self' is the mind's self-confusion, for mind is not an object that can be examined. However, when observed with authentic intelligence which is the self-manifestation of wisdom, then the primal original position of the basic ground, the heart of enlightenment, is authentically experienced, or is clearly seen, or is how one's mind abides.

SUTOSYO ME BHAVA The impure, confused state of mind known as 'I' binds together [i.e. reifies] all the basic elements of existence (skandhas, dhātus, ayutana). When karma and obscurations are purified just as iron is gradually turned to gold in alchemy, Vajrasattva becomes very happy.

SUPOSYO ME BHAVA With that purity, gradually all the many objects perceived by the mind from the situation of 'I' are sealed as the self-expression of the original knowing. And thus all possible appearances are experienced as the pure infinitude of the buddhas' modes and dimensions and one's own face is happily displayed to oneself.

ANURAKTO ME BHAVA All sentient beings, those who identify themselves as 'I', have gone under the power of the confusion of reification. May we truly connect with and receive your blessing of the effective power and ability to end our self-revealing faults and then empty all the three worlds of samsara.

SARVA SIDDHIM ME PRAYACCHA Please grant me the general attainments of the pacification of the eight and sixteen fears within the situation of awareness. And also please grant me the supreme attainment of gaining the level of four vidyadharas [*vipak, ayush, mahamudra, sahaja,* the highest levels of tantric attainment].

SARVA KARMA SUCA ME CITTAM SREYAM KURU Gaining both these attainments and gaining power over birth and death, by a great wave of activity may I be able to bring virtue and happiness to the hearts and minds of all sentient beings.

HUM indicates the vajra, the unchanging actual nature of the mind of all the buddhas.

HA HA HA HA HO indicates that the vajra of that unchanging mind has the nature of the five modes [natural, display, manifest, ultimate and integrated] and the five original knowings [infinite, mirror-like, equality, accurate perception, all-accomplishing].

BHAGAVAN SARVA TATHAGATA Regarding that unchanging actual nature of mind, it is the presence of the true nature of all the buddhas of the various families and so it is the symbol of the natural mode (*dharmakāya*) of the buddhas.

VAJRA MA ME MUNCA This symbolises the display mode (*sambhogakāya*) quality of all the buddhas.

VAJRI BHAVA MAHA indicates the ceaseless flow of benefit for others which is the compassionate manifest mode (*nirmanakāya*) of all the buddhas.

SAMAYASATTVA In this way, with a clear understanding of the ultimate meaning of the secret key points of the way of natural perfection, at this very moment I become a great being (*mahasattva*) possessing the adamantine confidence of freedom from fear.

AA indicates the original nature which is the ground of all that appears, the nature which is unborn, free of coming and going, going out or coming in.

These hundred letters represent the forty-two peaceful deities and the fifty-eight wrathful deities, and are the essence of the hundred families of the peaceful and wrathful ones. In essence they belong to the single family of Vajrasattva whose heart mantra is composed of these hundred letters.

Thus both the visualisation of the deity and the recitation of the mantra form the actual antidote which purifies the karma, afflictions and obscurations of all sentient beings. The sound of the mantra arises as the spontaneous manifestation of the compassion of all the buddhas of the three times. It washes like purifying water. It burns like flaming fire which cleanses and purifies. It drives out dirt like the wind and has the qualities of everything purificatory.

Furthermore, imagining that your entire body within and without is like a crystal container being washed with water so that all dirt and dust is removed, recite that hundred-syllable mantra and the short mantra (OM VAJRA SATTVA HUNG) for as long as you can. Then imagine that everything dissolves into light and then melts into you. You then melt into light and dissolve into Vajrasattva on the crown of your head. He then dissolves into his heart essence HUNG (ཧཱུྃ). The ◡ dissolves into the ཨ, then the ཨ dissolves into the ◌, then the ◌ dissolves into the ཥ, then the ◡ dissolves into ◦, then the ◦ dissolves into the ˄, then the ˄ vanishes like an insubstantial rainbow. Abide in the natural way of mind, the situation of emptiness free of conceptualisation.

Finally, recite the dedication of merit and the prayers of aspiration according to your way of practice.

REGARDING THE SIGNS THAT ONE'S ERRORS AND OBSCURATIONS HAVE BEEN PURIFIED: to actually experience or to have the feeling in a dream, however it might be, that one's body is being washed or that rain is falling, purifying the stains from one's body. Experiencing insects, worms, pus, rotten blood coming out of one's body, or sooty water, shining oil or steam emerging. Experiencing one's flesh falling away and then being restored, or coming out from a swamp or pond. Experiencing light radiating from one's body, or sweet smelling elixir issuing from one's body or environment. Experiencing oneself flying in the sky or wearing white clothes. If one has these experiences it is a sign that one's errors and obscurations have been purified. So one must practise strongly until one gains these signs.

b. *The potency of the effective application of the antidotes*

It is important to be diligent in practising expiation and purification whether it be according to the TANTRA OF STAINLESS EXPIATION which occurs in the TANTRA OF THE UNLOADED ELEPHANT found in the open tradition (bKa'-Ma) of the victorious perfectly enlightened one, or according to the SUPREME MODE OF ORIGINAL KNOWING or other such texts occurring in the profound treasures of Guru Padmasambhava.

In general it is important to practise virtue with one's body, voice and mind, to encourage others to practise virtue, and to be diligent in abandoning unvirtue.

In particular, one should be diligent in practising both the developing and perfecting systems. Also by abiding evenly in the natural way of the great perfection, this ultimate practice has the power to completely eradicate the causal ignorance of belief in a reified self which is the root of all that occurs in the three worlds of samsara. This is like holding up a lamp in a dark room, and so the supreme teachings should be practised with diligence.

Furthermore, one should be energetic in the methods of expiating error that are found in many different practices such as making holy statues, books and stupas, showing respect to the sangha, and being generous to the poor.

c. The potency of total renunciation

If you were to eat food that was mixed with poison and then came to realise it, you would experience a great fear that you were going to die from the poison. In similar fashion, when you remember the causal erroneous and unvirtuous actions you have done, a great fear of the consequences should arise in your mind. You should think as follows:

> "In all my lives during this beginningless samsara I have been a wrong-doer who has accumulated many, many errors. This is really true and definite. In front of those virtuous ones who are without error, I feel ashamed and these virtuous ones also experience me as a shameful person. So with great guilt and remorse I fully confess and expiate my errors. The result of the errors I have performed in the past is certain to be suffering – and I will have to experience it. Knowing this I must quickly confess and make vows to be pure.
>
> Not trying to hide these errors or keep them secret within my mind, I will confess before the refuge of my guru and the buddha, dharma and sangha, without hiding or keeping secret any of the errors I have done in the past, those I do now, and any that I might

think to do in the future. I and all sentient beings are ignorant and confused and it is certain that we will experience difficulties due to the actions we have carried out in our confusion. For the errors we have accumulated, we ask you holy ones to grant forgiveness. All these accumulated errors are actually illusory so please accept our expiating confession and quickly purify our errors and obscurations."

Pray like this repeatedly from your heart and make prayers of aspiration.

d. The potency of abandoning the return to error

"FROM THIS TIME ON, EVEN IF MY LIFE IS AT STAKE, I WILL NOT DO ANYTHING ERRONEOUS OR UNVIRTUOUS." It is most important to make a strong commitment to hold firm to this decision.

We must pray again and again to our guru and to the triple gem until we have a clear aspiration not to do the unvirtuous deeds that we used to do, until the habits of wanting to perform them no longer occur even in our dreams.

If one genuinely confesses using the expiating power of those four potent antidotes, then one's errors and lapses, both great and small, will be purified and will not be repeated – all the texts agree on this. But if one does not clearly decide not to do these things in future, then even if one fully applies the first three antidotes listed above, one's errors will be difficult to clear. If one were now to commit one single error, and knowing that one had the means to expiate the error by confession, were to rely on the power of confession to support the repetition of error, then one would never be able to clear one's errors.

Therefore wise, intelligent people make use of all four expiatory antidotes to clear all the errors they have committed and do not commit more errors in future, and so they avoid trouble. If they should do something very bad then the potency of expiation via the four potent antidotes will diminish in its effect. If foolish people commit even small errors, then due to not knowing how to expiate them, these small errors will always accompany them and they will have to deal with an accumulated mountain of errors.

3. The Results Gained from Purifying Errors

Hidden in the mud at the bottom of the ocean is a jewel, and if that jewel is recovered, washed, dried and then polished, it appears as the wish-fulfilling gem. Similarly, hidden within the adventitious obscurations of the afflictions[2] and the cognisables[3] is the primordial ground, the actuality of the heart of enlightenment. The method by which it is liberated[4] in its own place is through the four potent antidotes. If you do this essential practice with determination then by its power you will understand the process of your mind which is the basis for recognising original knowing. Then understanding will continue to develop and even the subtlest obscurations will be purified. Your good qualities will increase and all obstacles on the path to buddhahood will be pacified. Traversing the ten stages and the five ways, you will attain the primordial security.

5. The difficulties experienced when Errors are not Purified

Generally speaking, the behaviour of ordinary beings contains many causal unvirtuous actions so that it seems that the errors are too trifling to accumulate. However they do gradually accumulate, just as great oceans are formed by the accumulation of tiny drops of water. Thus one accumulates a mass of errors which cause one to revolve round and round in samsara, descending ever further till one moves only in the three lowest realms of animals, hungry ghosts and hells. From there it is very hard to rise to the three upper realms, let alone to gain liberation.

6. The Benefits of Expiating Errors

At the moment we live under the power of our former carelessness due to which we accumulated our mistakes and errors. However now and in the future, with the power of being careful, we can make fully expiating confession so that even if we have committed the grave five limitless errors, we will still be freed – this has been taught by the Buddha. For this the examples of Ananda, Angulimala, Sudarshana and Nanda are often given.

In accordance with this explanation intelligent people who have done little previous dharma practice, or who have had little hope of gaining significant meditation experience or realisation, should take as their first dharma pursuit this practice of purifying errors. Then their qualities will automatically appear, as when rust is removed from an iron mirror. So it is very important to really keep this effective system in your mind.

Notes

[1] Details of these categories of limitations are given in Chapter 1 of *Simply Being*.

[2] The obscuration of the afflictions refers to the deluding power of immersion in stupidity, attraction and aversion and all their derivative afflictions.

[3] The obscuration of the cognisables refers to the deluding power of identification with, and reliance on, concepts. This leads to the experience of living in a world constituted out of real entities that one has thought about.

[4] It is liberated from obscurations which have never obscured it. Primordially free and pure, it pervades all beings. Yet for them, in their ignorance it is like an essence inside them that has to be freed from ensnaring defilements.

6

Padmasambhava Introduces Himself

King Trisong Detsen (*Khri-Srong lDeu-Tsan*) thought,

"I am the king of the whole Tibet. Even the great Acharya Shanta-rakshita has bowed down to me. So now Acharya Padmasambhava should bow down to me."

Then Padmasambhava introduced himself:

"Salutation to the Guru and to Buddha, Dharma and Sangha. Listen to me, Tibetan King!

I am Padmasambhava, the son of all the Buddhas of the past, present and future. I have acquired merit for many kalpas, vast periods of time. Due to this, I have become Buddha Padma-sambhava.

I understand the entire Buddhist Philosophy. I have studied all the collected teachings, all the Pitakas and Agamas. I carry with me all the Mahayana Teachings. I am pure Dharma Padma-sambhava.

I have mastered all the practices and teachings of all the paths. Externally, I put on the dress of a monk. Internally, I am a yogi of the highest anuttara mantra vehicle. I am Sangha Padmasambhava.

The view, practices and teachings of dharma are with me. My knowledge is greater than nirvana. My vehicle is bigger than samsara. I am attentive to cause and effect and I perform no sin or unskilful activities. So I am Guru Padmasambhava.

I have teachings which always produce good results for those who come into contact with them. I explain both the literal and the spiritual sense of language and of all books. Thus I am spiritual friend, Kalayanmitra Padmasambhava.

I am in a position to give instructions on the nature of virtue and non-virtue. I put on the dress of intrinsic knowing. I have in my hand the bowl of the five modes of enlightened being. I am Abbot Padmasambhava.

I give advice to all living beings on the attainment of the balance and infinite radiance of nirvana. I abide in the meditations of the developing and completions stages. I am great practitioner Padmasambhava.

I give the same advice for both meditation and post-meditation experience. Samsara and nirvana are both within the Buddha's mandala. For me the developing and contemplation stages are the same. I am master of the view Padmasambhava.

I have mastered the instructions of the developing and completion stages and I control the red and white essences. With my knowledge I can calculate karmic cause and effect. I see the relation between all events. I am yogi Padmasambhava.

I have the non-dual understanding expressed in the Buddha's teachings. To those who suffer from the five afflictions I give the remedy of knowledge so that they recover. Those whom I revive gain the elixir of secret instruction from me. I am Medicine Guru Padmasambhava.

On the opaque sight of ordinary people I display clarity and emptiness. I am the artist Padmasambhava, and on the soft paper of the mind I express the integration of spaciousness, awareness and clarity without concept or language. For this I have with me religious instructions without letters[1]. So I am scribe Padmasambhava.

To people born in the four directions I make predictions about the future. I have knowledge of the future and I can reveal it. I have all religious instructions – whatever anyone require. Since the five afflictions have become the five enemies, I dissolve them into the five intrinsic knowings. So I am magician Padma-sambhava.

I possess the means to drive away the five afflictions. Without abandoning the pleasures of the five senses, I integrate them on the religious path. I enjoy them with the help of the five intrinsic knowings. So I am Bon-Po Padmasambhava.

I have with me instructions on how to transform inauspicious signs into good ones. I put the beings of the six realms into the realm of joy. I subdue all the eight classes of spirits including the local gods. Thus I am King Padmasambhava.

I have instructions which will discipline the beings of the three worlds. I know the nature of the karma of this world. I bring peace to the hearts of all beings. So I am minister Padma-sambhava.

I have with me instructions to turn the irreligious towards dharma. I work until all beings attain nirvana. I work for nirvana. I only see the Three Jewels and no others. So I am Three Jewels Padmasambhava.

I have with me advice to attain nirvana at the time of death. I work for the happiness of nirvana. I have with me instructions which can put an end to illusion and confusion. With the weapon of love and compassion I can kill dualistic perception. I am hero Padmasambhava.

I have with me the means to end the afflictions. I give three kinds of gifts: I teach the Dharma, I give charity, and I support those in distress. I establish all fortunate disciples in Dharma. Thus I am old Padmasambhava.

I wear the three-fold armour of tolerance: I do not consider the enemy to be enemy, I consider suffering as joy, and I know the real nature of Dharma and can stand it. I destroy the illusion of suffering. I am young Padmasambhava.

I have with me teachings which can establish the four obstructing Maras[3] in illusion. I inhabit the citadel of the three meditations: to have evaluation and intention in meditation, to have evaluation but no intention, to have no intention and no evaluation. Thus I am teenage Padmasambhava.

I have with me teachings to end all harm and I can see with the eyes of the three wisdoms: worldly wisdom, beyond worldly wisdom, and beyond worldly great wisdom. I drink the milk of actuality and intrinsic knowing. Thus I am child Padmasambhava.

I have teachings with me whereby one can sit and sleep and meditate and thereby gain liberation. All the beings in the three realms are impermanent. I have gained the level of the immortal vidyadhara, so I am immortal Padmasambhava.

I have teachings with me which are called secret instructions on the practice of indestructibility. My body has no connection with the four elements. My body was not born of flesh and blood, so I am unborn Padmasambhava.

I have with me Mahamudra teachings. My body is the indestructible vajra body so it cannot become old or be destroyed. My bodhicitta has no beginning or end, so I am ever-young Padmasambhava.

I have with me teachings for ending suffering. Young men's bodies can be spoiled by disease. Glowing health can also be destroyed by disease but I am Padmasambhava without any disease.

I have with me teachings of the great completion, Dzogchen.

You, the Tibetan King, stay in a barbarian country without any religion. You have a red body and your country is inhabited by rakshasa demons. You are the King of this country. You think that you have become very big in this world. You are full of attachment and self-cherishing. Grasping at yourself as being really existent and important is the cause of your birth in this world. Your body has the five afflictions as ornaments. You are the lord of Tibet but you stay in an unvirtuous land. Your servants and the ordinary people all eat meat. You have all the treasures of unvirtue. Seeing you, I do not feel happy and joyous.

Your wife has the appearance of a human being but in fact she is a demoness. All those who accompany your wife are demon girls of black and red complexion. They have gold, silk, and other ornaments on their bodies but they do not give any sense of joy and beauty.

O King! You only feel happy because you are King. Anyone who becomes your subject will want to die. You are very commanding and you want respect even from me. I do not bow down to you.

Yet, as a result of your past actions, I came here to Central Tibet on your invitation. O King! Come here. I do not bow down to you but I bow down to one of your robes."

Thus saying, Padmasambhava raised one finger of his right hand. The magic power radiating from his finger burnt all the robes of the King. Seeing this, all the people bowed down to him in respect.

Padmasambhava told the King that in order to cleanse all the sins committed by his body, he should build five stupas. The King built these as instructed.

Then on the first day of the first month of the autumn season, King Trisong Detsen invited Padmasambhava to Samye Monastery. When he arrived there, Mahacharya Padmasambhava was given a golden seat on the right hand side of the King. On the left hand side, a silver seat was given to Acharya Shantarakshita. Mahacharya Padmasambhava put on a robe which was brown coloured. He was given food and drink and many other offerings. He was also given gold, jewels and other precious items. Then the King explained that he was unable to complete the construction of Samye Monastery:

"Guru, divine manifestation, I am suffering from many difficulties. The people of Tibet also suffer. So in order to drive away suffering, a monastery must be built. To teach Buddhism, a temple must be built. Please lay the foundations for building on this land."

Padmasambhava agreed. He said that the land of Tibet resembled a rakshasa demon lying on the ground. Therefore a monastery nine stories high should be built. On the rakshasa demon's hands and legs a total of one hundred and eight stupas should be built. On the navel of the rakshasa demon a stupa should be built. He told them that in the Magro village there was a Naga King, Magrochen, who should be worshipped at the edge of the village where the streams meet.

These instructions ensured that the dharma was established in Tibet.

NOTES

[1] That is to say, instructions which cannot be spoken or written.

[2] The afflictions, death, desire and ego-inflation.

7

Padmasambhava: Meaningful to Behold

Princess Mandarava reached Tibet when a reception was being held for Padmasambhava. She praised him with the following words:

"Oh Great Master! When you teach for the good of the world you put on a hat with five peaks. This indicates that initiation in the five kāyas[1], the five modes of enlightenment, has been attained and the five branches of knowledge[2] are fully mastered.

The peak in the centre of your hat is blue which is the sign of the intrinsic knowing of infinite hospitality (*dharmadhātujñāna*). At the front is the white peak, the sign of mirror-like intrinsic knowing (*adarshajñāna*). On the left[3] is the yellow peak, the sign of the intrinsic knowing of open evenness (*samantajñāna*). At the back there is the red peak, the sign of discerning intrinsic knowing (*ratyaveksanajñāna*). To the right is the green peak, sign of the accomplishing intrinsic knowing (*krtyanusthanajñāna*).

For the good of the world you show the signs of the four activities of pacification, development, suppression and destruction. Your hat has images of three heads, a skull-head, a dried-up head and a fresh head as a sign that you give teachings without limit. Your hat is adorned with jewels as a sign of your being honoured in the three realms[4]. It has a golden vajra attached to it as the sign of your indestructible meditation. It has a diadem with symbols in the five colours with tassels attached to it, a sign of doing good in the world with the five intrinsic knowings. Your hat is decorated with feathers from the throat of a vulture, a sign of the union of wisdom (*prajna*) and skillful means (*upaya*). Standing upright on the top of the hat is a peacock's tail feather, a sign of the inseparability of clarity, spaciousness (*dhātu*) and awareness (*vidya*). It carries golden symbols of the sun and the moon, a sign that you drive away the darkness and ignorance (*avidya*) of the world. Pieces of deerskin have been folded at the corners as a sign that you employ tantra and sutra for the good of the world. The ends of the hat hang down as a sign that you see the nature of actuality.

Padmasambhava, when your body is seen you look like the Tathagata. You abide in ceaseless deep meditation (*samadhi*). Your body is white with a red tinge, showing that you are full of perfect happiness. Your eyes are focussed straight ahead, a sign of being merged in infinite space (*dharmadhātu*). Your face is smiling and you have beautiful teeth, a sign of the fulfilment of tantric action. Your voice teaches with the sixty tones of Brahma[5], a sign that you bring joy to all beings in the six worlds[6].

Five winds[7] flow from your nose as a sign that you are completely free of all conceptual elaboration. In your ears you wear golden rings with bells as a sign of direct communication with all the buddhas. Your hair is black and is tied up as a sign of being free of all disturbance. You sit in lotus posture as a sign of the fulfilment of the five ways (*marga*) and the ten stages (*bhumi*). Your left hand holds a skull-cup (*kapala*) as a sign of the enjoyment of worldly pleasures. In your right hand you hold a vajra as a sign of your practice of blissful emptiness (*ananda śūnyatā*).

At the elbow of your left hand there is a staff of water-tree wood[8] as a sign that you unite and perfect all dharmas in one vehicle (*yana*). In its middle there is a knot in the form of a leviathan (*makara*)[9] as a sign of the preservation of dharma by the four assemblies[10]. On the top of that staff there is a vajra with five tips as a sign of liberation from the four kinds of birth[11]. It has nine heads as a sign of meditation in the eight great cemeteries. It has a five-coloured cover as a sign of the integration of emptiness and the five intrinsic knowings[12]. Small bands in gold, silver, iron and copper are round it as a sign of the use of mantra as a means to benefit the world. A trident is fixed to it as a sign of your stability of body, voice and mind. At the top of the trident there are traces of three eyes as a sign of seeing the opening of actuality. From it hang eight iron rings as a sign of the purification of the eight consciousnesses[13].

On your body you wear a robe, a sign of prosperity arising from your practice. It is adorned with red, yellow, white and green threads, a sign of the clarity that arises from the natural mode of enlightenment (*dharmakāya*). The colour of the robe is blue and it is sewn with golden thread as a sign of unchangeable infinite spaciousness (*dharmadhātu*).

Padmasambhava, you were born on the tip of a lotus flower in a lake, which is a sign of being free of any worldly limitation. Rainbows surround you in the four directions, a sign of the dissolving of the components (*skandhas*)[14] and the attainment of Buddhahood. In your entourage you have many great teachers, a sign of your gift of ripening your fortunate disciples. Your body has been praised as having the thirty-two major and eighty minor signs of a Buddha's body."

Mandarava asked Padmasambhava:

"How can the people of the future whom you have not yet seen, remove their mental darkness? How can they gain merit through generosity? To whom should they offer their service? Who will remove the sorrow of the world? Who will bring happiness to this world? Who will continue your succession? Please tell us who will come after you in future to help us?"

Padmasambhava said:

"Listen, goddess who has assumed human form. In future people will worship my image and this will remove the sorrow of the world.

By making images of me, the vajrayana dharma which shows the three modes of enlightenment will triumph.

By paying homage to images of me, the desires of the people will be fulfilled as if by the wish-fulfilling gem.

By reciting prayers to me in front of my image, true value will be achieved.

By worshiping it with the activity of their five senses, their welfare will be secured.

By offering water with medicine in it to my image, the diseases of their bodies and all bodily inconveniences will disappear.

By people acting as priests towards my image, freedom from ghosts and the hells will be obtained and all necessary merit will be acquired.

By building temples for images of me, wise beings will be born.

By helping to make images, there will be teaching of the dharma.

By offering a place for image-making, they will become skilled in the five kinds of knowledge.

By giving clay for image-making, merit will increase.

By offering clothes for my image, they will gain knowledge as an ornament for themselves.

By offering a lotus seat for my image, soft and beautiful cushions will be obtained.

By cleaning dust from my temple, they will gain a beautiful form.

By worshiping my image with water, their bodies will be clean and beautiful.

By offering service or worship to my image, miracles will be achieved.

By worshiping it with lamps, they will be intelligent and the darkness of ignorance will disappear.

By worshiping my image with jewels, poverty will vanish and they will be rich.

By worshiping it with incense, they will be fragrant.

By worshiping it with medicine, diseases will vanish and they will be immortal.

By offering the five precious substances[15] to my image, their sorrow will vanish.

By offering water for cleaning it, pure places will be established.

By giving food offerings, hunger will vanish and pleasure will come.

By offering vegetables, they will be cleansed and purity will be attained.

By offering milk and ghee, they will enter the desire realms.

By offering honey and sugar, they will gain all they desire.

By offering visual objects, their merit will increase.

By offering wealth, clothes and ornaments will be obtained.

By offering a gong, they will have a sweet voice.

By offering small gongs, they will be powerful.

By offering prostrations, they will gain liberation in this life.

By applying golden colour to my image, they will become princes.

By applying silver colour to my image, they will become queens.

By applying shellac colour to my image, the most beautiful horse will be born for them.

By applying copper colour to my image, they will become government ministers.

By applying red colour to my image, they will get jewels.

By offering the sap of trees, they will get the wheel of the universal emperor.

By offering seven jewels, they will be able to see the enjoyment mode of enlightenment, sambhogakāya.

By writing and reading my life story, they will understand fully the meaning of infinite space and awareness.

By installing images, war, disease, calamity and so on will disappear. Images of Padmasambhava will send forth light.

For the benefit of future generations these images are like the wish-fulfilling jewel.

Those who are like my children should pray to me. You should circumambulate my image with a pure heart. If you pray to me you will be free from sorrow caused by ghosts, and you will live in pleasure.

Those who are poor should pray to me. They will get riches.

Those whose wishes have not been fulfilled should pray to me, for their wishes will then be fulfilled."

Notes

1 The five kayas (sKu-lNga) are dharmakaya, sambhogakaya, nirmanakaya, vajrakaya and abhisambodhikaya.

2 The arts, grammar, medicine, logic and dharma.

3 Left and right are as they appear to an observer looking from the front.

4 The realms of desire, form and formlessness.

5 Brahma is said to have a voice the tones of which bring multiple worlds into existence.

6 The worlds of gods, jealous gods, humans, animals, hungry ghosts and hell beings.

7 The winds which control swallowing, respiration, digestion, excretion and energy.

8 Water-tree wood is wood without a core and can refer to bamboo or plantain but in this case it is referring to the black palm tree [Borassus flabellifer] which is very hard and non-absorbent, despite its having a soft core.

9 This sea monster can swallow anything and is a symbol of emptiness.

10 Monks, arhats, nuns, and lay men and women.

11 Womb, egg, heat and moisture, and miraculous.

12 See the description in paragraph 3 of this chapter.

13 Of seeing, hearing, smelling, touching, tasting, mentation, afflicted mentation, base of everything.

14 Form, feelings, perception, assumptions and tendencies, and consciousness.

15 Gold, silver, turquoise, coral and pearl.

8

Padmasambhava's Predictions

Padmasambhava arranged for the Treasure Doctrines (*gTer*) to be hidden that they might be revealed later when the bad signs and calamities of the Kali Yuga, the present dark and degenerate age, increase.

"Regarding the occasions when the treasures will be revealed by the appointed treasure revealers, Tertons (*gTer-sTon*), they will appear at the time of calamity and at the time of the overthrow of Kings, when the subjects become unhappy and the country declines.

Due to anger, war occurs. Due to desire, the country faces evil times. Due to extreme stupidity, disease appears. Everyone becomes unhappy. At that time a master will appear and he will teach about mantras, rituals, astrology and medicine. These teachings will be revealed from hidden treasure and will be made use of as and when necessary."

For example,

"At Lato in Western Tibet a Terton will be born when there is calamity and disease.

On the border of Tibet and Nepal, a Terton will be born when men will be burned in forests.

In Khenke at Lendo, a Terton will be born when there will be quarrels inside the temple in the years of the dog and the bird.

In Manyul, a Terton will be born when the sky will become red and red rain drops for eighteen months causing drought.

In Shot Shun, a Terton will be born when many people die and there is no place to bury them."

Padmasambhava made the following predictions regarding the bad signs that would arise:

"In Tibet due to war waged by Mongolians, parts of Tibet will go under Mongolian occupation. People will start putting on iron armour.

Among two sects there will be quarrels and religion will face schism.

The roof of the temple built by Tri Ratna will be blown off by wind and the sun's rays will enter into the temple.

China's capital will be taken by the people Tai Ching. Tibet's buddhism will prosper and the prestige of the Tibetan government will increase.

At that time Tibetan people acquire arms and the throne will go to the hands of the people.

In Upper Tibet, tents will disappear with the wind. At that time in Tibet there will be three sects [Nyingma, Kagyu, Sakya]. Buddhism will spread through the Buddha's teachings and through revealed treasure teachings.

Religious people will enact the afflictions [stupidity, anger, desire, jealousy, pride]. Through the spread of false dharma, buddhism will be destroyed.

In all the places of pilgrimage, forts will be constructed. In Lhasa on the summit of the red hill, there will be a temple [Potala]. The lake near the red hill will dry up and will be filled with sand.

Saying, 'I am the incarnation of Padmasambhava', people will practise false dharma.

People of South Tibet will have to leave their country. Laymen resort to magic. Those who practise tantric sadhanas also practise magic. When human beings die, there will be offerings of books. When people move from village to village they will have to go in groups.

Tibet will be broken into pieces and places of pilgrimage will be owned by many groups. The King of Purang will demand gold from Tibet[1].

Tibetan people start translating Indian texts even without going to India. Tibet's best scholars will be taken away to Mongolia. Inside Tibet will be darkness and in other countries there will be light. Tibetan dharma and fortune will go down.

The Sakyapa sect will come to Tibet with Mongolian soldiers.

When the war drum is sounded, people will throw away their treasures, including gold.

Inside the temple, offerings for gods will be given to horses. Zho-Long village will burn with fire. At Pal-Trog village, pipe-guns will be used.

In Silne village, a tree having the shape of a man will come into being. In Manda village, stone for making mirrors will appear.

Kings will start feeding the Mongolian people. Mongolian people will make a monk elder a general.

Sakya and Ting will spoil their power in the end due to prolonged struggle.

From day to day the times will become more troublesome. Some yogis will become abbots and, going to villages, will give initiation and conceal girls. As a result of quarrels, deaths are caused indirectly.

False buddhism will make its appearance. Evil will appear as religion. Fake medicine will be made and shorten life. New astrology will be full of errors.

The religion of Tibet will become some sort of sport. Laymen will also preach. Laymen will say that there is no difference between a yogi and a layman. People not connected with religion will start preaching.

The five non-reliances[2] will arise. All will become untrustworthy. Many diseases will appear and people will discard their local dress.

In Tibet, people will wear new kinds of clothes. They will practise different forms of religion. In the monasteries all the pictures will be spoilt.

In Sakya village, a deer will be born and due to ill luck that deer will come and kill human beings.

As a result of quarrels, yogis will die and the stone stupa near Samye Monastery, built at the time of Padmasambhava, will be destroyed.

Even without practising meditation rituals, people will claim to be tantric practitioners. Many will claim to have attainments. Even without having received initiation oneself, initiation will be offered to others.

In Central Tibet, people will become united and so Sakya and Mongolians will become afraid. Evil and demons will reign supreme.

A sinful king will be born. Phag-Mo, as King, will conquer Central and Eastern Tibet and will build one hundred and eight forts.

Mongolian and Sakya will fight against each other and the dead will be buried in Bi and Tsang villages. Foreigners will come, Phagmo and Drigung will fight along with foreigners and Bi and Tsang villages will be divided. Human skulls will be brought out from inside the stupa by dogs[3].

Ken and Tong of the Tsang village will fight among themselves. After that Relong and Tsulong will be occupied by soldiers.

A man will be born. He will bring foreign soldiers to Tibet. He will introduce fighting among friends.

False religion will prevail. The prestige of men and gods will decline in Tibet.

On the hill of the Kharak village, there will be strict surveillance among people.

In Ngagmat village, a fort will be built. One hundred and sixteen military officers will assemble at Tsalong.

In Yanlong, there will be military cantonment. In Tangtok two kinds of the military men will die.

In Genphu, soldiers of Phagmo Drupa (*Phag-Mo Gru-Pa*) will arrive. In Toklong province, the same military personnel will come and all the places will be occupied.

In Phagningshe, a fort will be built. In Ladakh, there will be a festival of poison. In Tibet, the Indians Kamaripa and Vimala will come and worship Buddha images in Lhasa.

People from the village will take shelter in the hills, and there will be calamity.

In Central Tibet, there will be a festival and the temple of Hepun will catch fire.

The world will be full of troubles. No peace will be there.

Just as the sun shines after the rain, a great man will appear in the form of a Terton, and taking ter [treasure] will do good for the world. In one decade only one Terton will appear. Sometimes great Tertons will appear, sometimes small ones will appear."

Padmasambhava told of the indications for the appropriateness of revealing the treasure.

"Righteous people will perform sins.

People wear black blankets made out of yak's tail.

The outside of the monasteries are fenced by soldiers.

Retreats are burnt with fire.

People make trade with the Buddha's sayings and books.

People use dharma books to pay compensation for having beaten people.

Yogis work for soldiers and they put on iron armour, whilst great saints become generals.

Bhikshus are killed.

Battle grounds are prepared in places of pilgrimage.

All the retreat places are made into cities.

Tantricas quarrel among themselves.

Poison is put in food to kill people.

The chief does not keep his words.

The hero looks like a sportsman.

The whole of Tibet will be split like fragments of iron armour.

Father and son will quarrel amongst themselves.

Relatives beat each another.

Ghosts and spirits are worshipped.

Robbers haunt the roads and snatch things from others.

Evil spirits enter the body of male persons.

Rakshasa [cannibal demons] enter the body of female persons.

Invited ghosts will enter the bodies of children.

All beings will go under the power of demons [mara].

All the eight groups of spirits such as deva [worldly gods] and rakshasa [cannibal demons] will fight among themselves. For these reasons people will suffer from diseases.

At that time three things will happen:

It will be impossible to keep minerals inside the earth.

The Tri Ratna [Buddha, Dharma and Sangha] treasures cannot be kept. The dharma is spoilt and devotees cannot do anything.

Without doing their own practice, people will give instructions to others."

After the death of the Queen's daughter, Padmasambhava told King Trisong Detsen about these future events.

"This great monastery built by the King will be destroyed. The King will die in the sixtieth year of the cow. In the end Mongolian people will come to Tibet. Buddhism will have vicissitudes and Tibet will suffer from time to time."

The King asked,

"Who is going to take this throne?"

Padmasambhava told him:

"After one hundred and twenty years have elapsed, Chinkun King's rules will be observed in Tibet. In the end the Chinkun will quarrel among themselves and the Chinese will come. From the Manchu country the incarnation of Manjushri will rule for some time. As in Sadia, the Chinese will come digging the earth. In the Yarlong there will be an incarnation of Vajrapani. In the year of the cow the Mongolians will again come to Tibet. The whole of Eastern Tibet will be conquered by them.

If I say much, you will feel sad. If the sixteen cities are destroyed, there will be some peace. The Chinese palace will be destroyed by four bhuta demons. The life of the people will be unsafe. Property will not be traced. Mongolians will come inside Tibet. Eighteen generations will survive.

The king will die in the fiftieth year of the tiger and will suffer much."

Then the king asked to be told more.

"After two generations the virtues of the Tibetan people will come to an end. Langdarma (gLang-Dar-Ma) will appear like an animal. Another will come with a monkey's head. They will kill big people, drive away small people and will destroy buddhism.

The virtuous people will be killed and the whole monastery will be desecrated. The people's virtues will be spoilt. People will indulge in vice. The King's laws[4] will disappear leaving chaos. Parents will be killed by their own children. This is called Kali Yuga, the dark age.

Langdarma will be beaten by Lhalung Palgyi Dorje. Langdarma will rule for one year and one month. At that time Bodhisattva Lhalung Palgyi Dorje will shoot an arrow to preserve buddhism.

The dynasty of Srongtsen Gampo (Srong-bTsan sGam-Po) will go to Ladakh and after eight generation in Nari [in Ladakh]. In the village of Purang, there will be three sons in the royal family.

Monasteries will be destroyed. Monasteries built by Srongtsen Gampo and others will be desecrated by pigeons.

In Mongolia, Srikunta will be the King. In the year of the iron dog there will be a rain of weapons and tulku lama emanations will have to quit Tibet. In Central Tibet, Mongolians will occupy and issue orders.

Mongolian law will be destroyed. After one hundred and twenty years years Chinkun laws will prevail. But during the Tsang dynasty the Chinese will come to an end.

In the year of iron dog, Mongolians will come to Tibet and in the year of the water horse, they will run. In the year of fire and cow, people will suffer. In the year of the lamb, Mongolians will go back but there will be terrible destruction. People's lives will be like a meteor. People will not have prosperity and will reap bad harvests.

War will spoil everything and there will be a sea of blood."

The causes of suffering are then described as follows:

"Mara made an aspiration at the time of the Buddha's victory that everything would come into his , Mara's, hands after the Buddha's time. That aspiration was made in the Buddha's presence. Due to this aspiration, at the end of the Buddha's time bhuta [demons] will enter the minds of virtuous people and the Buddha's dharma will come to an end.

Tibet is in the Himalayas. There was a spirit called Megan Dempo. His family survived in Tibet. His father was called Rinchen. He gathered his possessions in a bag made of leather. In the year of iron and tiger, there will be born a son in that family. He will cheat and increase suffering in the country.

In the years of rat, dragon and monkey, Chinese soldiers will come to Tibet. In the years of water and monkey, in the Yanlong village, there will be a meeting and cannon balls will be fired. In the year of the rabbit, the whole area will be spoilt. In the south there will be Chinese camps. All the Tibetans in Mongolia will suffer much. The Lungche Go monastery will be destroyed and bad characters will abound."

Selected and translated by C.R. Lama

Notes

[1] This was the gold that had been collected in order to invite Atisha from India.

[2] Wife not trusting own husband; yogi not keeping promises; people losing trust; father and son not trusting each other; teacher and disciple not trusting each other.

[3] One skull belonged to Acharya Shantarakshita. He had previously been buried under a stupa and later the stupa broke into pieces and dogs brought out his skull.

[4] The laws of King Srongtsen Gampo (*Srong-bTsan sGam-Po*).

© Shelley & Donald Rubin Foundation

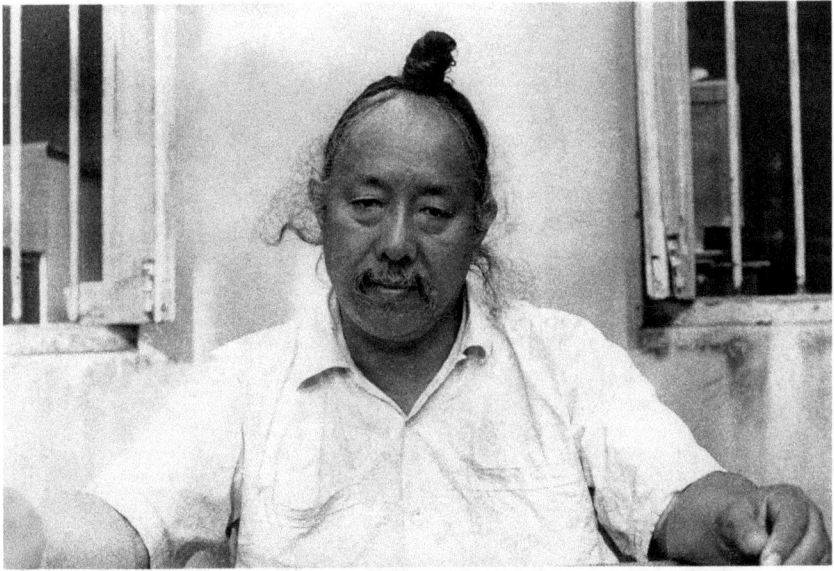

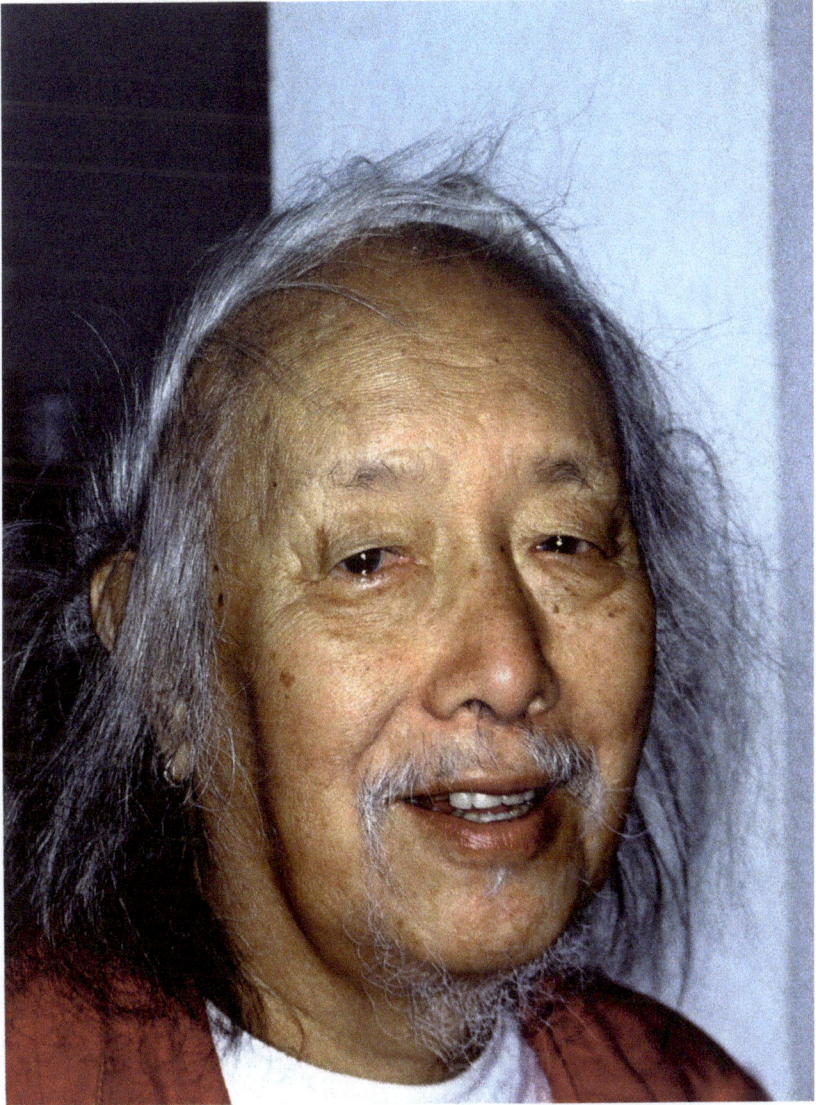

9

Extracts from Prefaces

Lhadrub Guruyoga, 1981

People say that they have a root Guru, some particular Lama who is like that and like this, with such and such qualities. Some say that their root Guru is a well-known Guru, while others say that their root Guru is a young Lama who looks very nice. An old Guru is also a Guru and a young Guru is also a Guru – if they are Gurus.

In Sanskrit the word 'Guru' has two meanings, a qualified religious teacher, and beef. In both cases the idea is of heaviness. Beef is heavy food with many vitamins and after eating it one feels sleepy. A Guru who is qualified is also heavy, weighty with many good qualities. In any event the Guru is important but it is up to the disciple himself to develop very strong faith and really believe in his Guru. If one practises like that, results will be gained.

Three days ago I met someone who told me that he had received a particular initiation from one Lama. But I know that this was impossible since that practice belongs to one sect and the Guru to another and this Guru is personally known to me to practise only the teachings of his own sect. Thus in this way those who have no real Guru deceive themselves and cheat others.

In these times Gurus must practise according to their own religious texts and follow their own Guru's orders performing the work they are told to do. I do not say this for high Gurus but for ones similar to myself. I do not call myself a Guru but some people believe me to be one.

All the five sects of Tibet require a Guru Puja; the Gelug focus on Tsongkhapa, the Sakya focus on Sakya Pandita, the Kagyu focus on Naropa or Marpa, the Bonpo focus on Tonpa Shenrab and the Nyingma focus on Padmasambhava. Yet it seems to me that although the words are different, the practices and the ideas are the same. Some of these systems show the Guru in the form in which he appeared in Tibet when an image or painting was made while he was alive. We do not have an accurate picture of Buddha Shakyamuni. Not only that, but in some systems of practice the Guru is in the form of Lama Chemchog Heruka or Tara or Naljorma.

In other systems the Guru is in the form of Kuntuzangpo or Dorje Chang or Dorje Cho. These are three names for the integration of Dharmakāya, Sambhogakāya and Nirmanakāya. Kuntuzangpo or Samantabhadra is Dharmakāya form. Dorje Chang or Vajradhara is Sambhogakāya form. Dorje Cho or Vajradharma is Nirmanakāya form. These forms are methods for expressing the Buddha's qualities, they are synonyms for his qualities. Kuntuzangpo means always good, Dorje Chang means always having tantric power and Dorje Cho means that the natural dharma is indestructible.

Sometimes we say Guru, or Lopon (sLob-dPon) meaning teacher, the one who explains what is not known to us. Sometimes we say Pachig (Pa-gCig) meaning father, for just as a father gives his wealth to his son, so the Guru gives initiations and profound secret teachings to his disciples. The Guru sometimes calls the disciple Thukse (Thugs-Sras) heart son, or Lobu (sLob-Bu) disciple son. The Guru and the disciple work together, on the one side there is compassion and on the other side, firm faith. Compassion is like a hook and the disciple's faith gives it something to catch on to – but they have to come together to be effective.

If one practises Guruyoga with a one-pointed mind, with faith, and sings with a good melody, then one's voice will move other people's minds and lead them to enter the Buddhadharma. I say that you should all practise Guruyoga once a day. If every day it is necessary to eat food, why is it not necessary also to say prayers?

Those yogis of unchangeable mind, ones with real faith and belief, may do the practice of Gurupuja on their Gurus in any form what-soever, whether monk or tantrika or saint or very ordinary form. They can meditate on their Guru as he is in his ordinary flesh body. But now in this Black Period every sentient being has a changeable mind and is not pure. Perhaps they have faith today but then tomorrow it has gone, or there are doubts. For this reason we should meditate on our Gurus in the form of Buddhas, Bodhisattvas, Wishing Gods, Padma-sambhava and so forth. To practise using the forms of the Gurus who came in former times is perhaps necessary nowadays since, having passed away, they cannot say any things that are difficult for the disciple to understand.

Lastly, I say that to talk about the root Guru is not enough – prayer and faith is important.

Khandro Thugtig, 1978

In the present Black Period, we people who believe in Buddha and Padmasambhava are so few in number. We have great faith in Padmasambhava's predictions, made when he was in Tibet and written down at that time by Yeshe Tsogyal and so on. These were later revealed and written down by the great Terton treasure revealers without being mixed with any falsities, [only true incar-nation Tertons could find them].

At this time in Tibet, the Land of Snows where Padmasambhava taught the dharma and gave initiation in Tibetan, the outer show forms of artificial religious practice have been destroyed. We feel very sad that Buddhism in Tibet has declined to this state of affairs. The true dharma is indestructible and is not affected by the actions of those in the current Black Period who make a show of being nice but are empty within, like the banana and bamboo trees. They are only debating and not meditating.

When we receive the initiations we say that we will always keep our vows but we know that to keep all our vows is not easy.

Brief Explanation of Refuge and Bodhicitta, 1979

I and other Tibetan teachers must be careful when giving refuge, bodh-icitta vows, initiations and tantric vows. Those who are giving them must have all the teaching practice and qualities that are necessary and keep their vows fully. It is necessary for them to explain clearly to those who are receiving just exactly what it is that is being given to them and what commitments and responsibilities they are taking upon themselves. For example, if a man is sick and in need of treatment and yet is himself unaware of his condition, then the doctor must be careful to explain the facts of the matter to him and the benefits of the treatment so that the sick man will be free of all suspicion that the medicine might in fact be a poison.

Compilation of Chod texts, 1978

Everything is coming from śūnyatā nature and goes back in that nature. Śūnyatā's symbol is zero. On the outside there is no corner and within there is hole with no corner. This śūnyatā dharmadhātu is everywhere equal, everywhere clear, everywhere precise under-standing, everywhere performing all activities unobstructedly.

This nature is śūnyatā. Sometimes we say dharmadhātu, dharmatā, dharmakāya and dharmadhātujñāna, but anyway, if you wish some symbol word then it is A (ཨ). This is the symbol of the Great Mother of all the Jinas, Gyalwa'i Yum Chenmo. Her nature is śūnyatā and all female beings also have that nature of śūnyatā. [But we do not say that śūnyatā means empty and idealess as in the common view of women held in former times. For every hundred mothers at least ninety will be equal in their attitude towards their children whether they are sons or daughters, first or last. But for those that are weak they will feel even more compassion.]

From sutra position the Mother is śūnyatā or tongpa nyid (sTong-Pa-Nyid). That śūnyatā has two aspects, outer and inner, Phyi sTong-Pa-Nyid and Nang sTong-Pa-Nyid. Or it may be considered as eighteen or as twenty-one śūnyatās.

What is discussed here is only śūnyatā. For this we can say only śūnyatā or zero and this is perhaps difficult for those who are not so intelligent.

Now we speak of Chod (gCod) which means to cut. To understand this we have to think clearly as follows. What is to be cut? Cut 'you' or cut 'I'? If I cut you that is sin and if I cut my own body that also is sin. But actually what is to be cut is my ego. Why? Because since beginning's time ego has made too much trouble for me. This bad ego has thrown me about sometimes in hells, sometimes amongst insatiable ghosts and so on. Where does ego come from? It comes from ignorance. Ignorance makes me and keeps me stupid and due to this I say subject and object, me and you, I am good and you are bad, I love me and I hate you. It is my ego that holds my body to be substantially real and then goes grasping through my flesh eyes. So then if I see something good there is desire, if something bad then anger, and if something better than I have then envy and so on. It is the same for ear, tongue, nose and bodily sensations. For that reason I must cut my ego. It is very bad and troublesome yet it cannot be seen with the flesh eye. It must be cut off and finished.

This teaching also deals with the great difficulties involved in getting a precious human birth. It is very difficult to get yet with it one can move easily, either up with good deeds or down due to sin. Up and down, round and round, just like a carnival wheel – yet there is a chance to get free.

Then there follows refuge, bodhicitta and making the outer and inner offerings and then the innermost offering of one's own body. After this one visualizes Machig Labdron with all her circle, all Gurus, all Devas and all Dakinis, and all the lineage Gurus around her. We pray to them so that they will bless us by cutting the root of egoism. Following this there is the transferring of the mind (*Pho-Ba*) by which one's mind goes to a very good place, merging in Machig's mind.

Then one transforms one's body into amrita for the four classes of guests: 1) the Buddhas and Bodhisattvas, 2) those with good qualities, the Lords with power placed below the first group, 3) all beings in the six realms, 4) all one's creditors. By offering to the first group the Buddhas are pleased. By offering to the second group one gains more qualities. By offering to the third group all sins are finished. By offering to the fourth group all debts are paid off.

Then one's body turns into jewels and so forth and these are offered to the gods of the samsaric heavens. Then one's body is also cut up and offered as a great mass of flesh and blood and bones and offered to all the local gods and demons who like such things. Then the remains are given to all the weak and disabled beings and by this all their troubles are removed. Then this practice concludes with the dedication of merit.

Machig Labdron was a great meditator and she might be called the Tibetan Nagarjuna. Nagarjuna taught śūnyatā but *she* taught how to separate our minds from ego. She stayed at Zangri Karmar, a red mountain near the Brahmaputra River about 500 miles to the east of Samye Monastery. When I went there and saw the stupa containing her remains I had a great feeling moving in my mind. I also remembered how my first incarnation Drophan Lingpa was formerly Machig's son, Gyalwa Dondrub.

By the virtue of making this translation we would like all beings to have their minds freed of egoism and thus to become equal. We would like all beings to gain full enlightenment and for the whole of samsara to be completely emptied.

When this translation was being done we said many prayers so perhaps it is free of mistakes but if there are any due to stupidity and ignorance and thus our vows have been lost, then we ask the Chod Protectors, the Zangri Punyi to excuse us.

But if these Chod Protectors do not excuse us then I also laugh at them. Right and wrong – everything is within śūnyatā. I also make this translation in order to spread the Dharma in the world. If you Dharma Protectors say this Dharma is not to be spread in the world then I tell you that you are jealous and tight-fisted. Dharma and Terma teachings are for all beings, not just for one particular area. If there is no virtue here then we dissolve it in śūnyatā.

10

Brief Teachings

1 Stay on the one point of presence

The main point of all Dzogchen teaching is that everything is empty. Emptiness, or śūnyatā, is the ground of all experience. Many different words are used to describe it but it is always the same. Whatever we hear or see or touch or taste or smell or feel or think is simply emptiness which is both empty and radiant. Recognising that all these are manifestations of the empty ground, our grasping at them as being something truly real stops.

If you have a body, then you have eyes and ears. When you die eyes and ears no longer function but the mind is still present. When alive, I am Mr A, but when I die, the dead body is Mr A. Mind always has the same nature, it is empty and open whatever occurs.

What comes in the mind arises due to some reason. For example, what I see is already filtered. I say, *"This is my friend, or my enemy"*, *"It is good or bad."* Similarly through the ear, I say the sound is sweet or not. What we hear evokes many different ideas, maybe with desire, maybe with anger.

At that moment don't look for future thoughts and don't go after past thoughts, just stay in the middle. For example, if you suddenly think, *"I want my enemy to die"*, don't try to antidote this 'bad' thought with a 'good' thought. Just leave it there. Don't grasp after any movement that comes into the mind, just stay on this one point of presence and leave the movement to do what it will. This is *Rig-Pa Rang-Grol*, self-liberating awareness. Awareness naturally comes free by itself in the Dharmakāya. It is never caught, never trapped.

First thought, not stop

Next thought, not wait for

Hold middle point

Always keep original nature

All Jinas go that way.

[Three months before he died the son of Dudjom Lingpa wrote this for C.R. Lama]

2   Empty nature

If you see all things clearly while knowing their nature is empty, then you will always be happy. However if you know the good qualities of something, for example your house, but do not know that it is empty of inherent self-nature, then you will be very sad if it burns. If the partner you love dies, there is sorrow but if you know the empty nature of all phenomena, then you will be happy. Appearance and emptiness are naturally joined and in their union is much joy.

Infinite space which offers all-encompassing hospitality, dharma-dhātu, is like a ball with no division or end. It has not been made by anyone, neither by Buddhas nor ourselves. It has no beginning and no end and is without differentiation. Nothing is separate from it and it is the depth and expanse of wisdom. It is free of giving and taking, allowed and not allowed, and within it everything arises free of grasping. It is great from the very beginning, pure and complete. Our own mind, our awareness, is inseparable from this great sky-like empty expanse. We are not a thing that can be grasped and we have no need to grasp.

Our awareness is pure from the very beginning, inseparable from the Dharmadhātu, free of centre and boundary. Uncontrived and without beginning or end, it is the depth of intrinsic knowing, free of accepting and rejecting, it is the great self-arising nature free of grasping. Primordially complete and pure, it is the realm of natural purity. We offer this continuously in the situation of effortlessly arising clarity.

3 Your own awareness is king

Your own awareness (*Rang-Rig*) is like a king. Why? If you recognise the nature of your mind, this is the source and ground, the original stage or situation, and then everything comes free by itself, both what we take to be object and what we take to be subject. Thus the mind is the main thing. It is the king.

Openness or emptiness (*śūnyatā, sTong-Pa-Nyid*) is like the sky, it is everywhere. It is our basic nature. It is free of interpretive concepts (*sPros-Bral*) simple and direct. It has no bias or attitude or limited viewpoint (*Phyogs-Ris-Med*). Emptiness is the nature of all-encompassing space (*dharmadhātu*) and this depth and expanse is unlimited in all directions. It cannot be found anywhere; it has no origin and it never vanishes (*'Ong-gNas-'Gro-Med*) – open unchanging awareness that is uninvolved with anything which occurs.

In order to get a result, effort must be made but this depends on karma and capacity. We need to have a hook which lets us hold on to the object of our practice until it becomes stable and the natural situation is revealed.

Ordinary karmic results give an intention which is like a lead hook – it bends easily.

If some effort is added to this then it is like a copper hook.

If you practise Dharma according to your own idea but with no Guru this is like a silver hook.

If you have faith and effort and a good Guru who has power and compassion then it is like a steel hook.

True dharma is precisely emptiness, our original nature. Taking refuge in this will never lead to trouble but not understanding emptiness can lead to confusion in Dharma practice.

4 Space

Buddhahood or Bodhi or enlightenment is awakening to your natural purity. Bodhicitta is the development of this experience, developing awareness of the primordial buddhahood of all beings. This also offers space to others which allows their own natural enlightenment to blossom and shine forth.

The ocean has great depth and stillness and also vast movement – neither aspect harms the other. The sky is vast and empty and in it many things move. Mind is vast and empty and in it many thoughts move. These movements cause no harm or trouble unless they are taken to be something real and separate in themselves.

5   Bodhi

The Sambhogakāya is reflected Bodhi – it is glorious and beautiful. It is not Bodhi itself since Bodhi has no form. The Sambhogakāya is the shining empty reflection of the Dharmakāya which is emptiness itself, inseparable from awareness. Dharmadhātu is the ground of the Dharmakāya. Dhātu, space, is like unworked gold – infinite potential. Dharmakāya, our natural enlightened mode is like a statue made of gold – from the unmoving openness it arises as a single point. This ends all the confusion of duality.

6   Bring about the result

Three causal factors operate to bring about the result. These are the root cause, the support and the secondary cause or circumstances. From them comes the result. For example, tea, sugar and milk is the cause. The pot is the support. The fire is the secondary cause. The tea is the result. Or, for weaving, yarn is the principal cause, the loom is the support, the weaver's skill is the secondary cause, and the cloth is the result. Or, for murder, stupidity and anger are the cause, an enemy is the support, a knife is the secondary cause and killing is the result.

The object of your desires is what you want, what is important to you, what you focus your attention on. Seeing needs an object, things which are visible. Hearing needs an object, things which are audible. Touching needs an object, things which are tangible. Tasting needs an object, things which are taste-able. Smelling needs an object, things which are smell-able. Mentation needs an object, things which can be apprehended by the mind.

There is an object which is attended to (*Yul*) and a subject who does the attending (*Yul-Can*). The relation between them is one of attention. When we work there has to be a base that we work on and proceed from. The basis is that which is attended to. If there is no basis there is no growth, no fruit. The object (*Bya-Yul*) is what you, the agent (*Byed-Pa-Po*) work on (*Bya-Ba*). In samsara the subject is always in a dualistic relationship with an object. The subject comes into being through relating to the object. They are inseparable. In relative truth practice we work to alter the relation between subject and object. In absolute truth there is no object, no subject and no relation between them.

7 Descriptions

Describing is also creating. *Kun-Tu brTag-Pa* means to identify an object, saying, *"It is this"*, *"It is that."* We both see and think, *"It is this"*, *"It is that."* When we are fully committed (*Yongs-Grub*) to this then what we see by relying on our flesh eye seems to be things which are complete in themselves, self-existing entities. For example we might say of a design that it is three-cornered, blue and beautiful. We seem to be seeing its qualities as existing in themselves out there. We can also say this of images in dreams. This capacity for description can be harnessed by both awareness (*Rig-Pa*) and by ignorance (*Ma-Rig-Pa*). When we experience our description inseparable from emptiness, this is the energy or creativity of awareness (*Rig-Pa'i-rTsal*). When we grasp at what we describe and take it to be self-existing this is the ignorance of identification (*Kun-Tu-brTag-Pa'i Ma-Rig-Pa*).

8 Signs

We rely on signs to make sense of our experience. The ground of the sign (*mTshan-gZhi*) is the basis for building meaning; it is the object or ground we build on. This is grasped with the sign (*mTshan-Ma*) which is like the strength of the land, its shape and qualities. On the basis of this we have identification (*mTshan-Nyid*). This is like the materials with which the walls and door and roof of a house are made. This is what makes it a house. If it were made of cloth it would be a tent, thus the identification defines the particularity of what is there. When practice is done physically the person who practises gains qualities (*mTshan-bCas*), for example through the practice of breath control (*rTsa-rLung*). With direct experience, not resting on the body, there is awareness beyond the identification of qualities (*mTshan-Med*) as in Dzogchen. With *mTshan-bCas* there is a model which can be followed and you know by comparing and contrasting if it is right. With *mTshan-Med* there is no model. Experience is unique. It is as if someone makes something that seemed completely strange and unknown; it cannot be understood by comparing and contrasting but only directly with the clarity of the natural situation.

9 Grasping

Grasping (*bDag-'Dzin*) is an enemy for it makes trouble for us. Grasping grasps at entities which it itself creates and sustains. It is a deluded and deluding activity arising from the reification which mistakes the illusory nature of phenomena. Grasping is not a thought nor is it an object, yet it can taint and confuse both thoughts and objects. This grasping ego, the sense of I, me, myself, must be killed by the mind itself, for the mind's nature is free of grasping. It is 'killed' by relaxing, by opening to the spacious source of the mind, by releasing the energy invested in grasping so that grasping dissolves in space, like morning mist into the sky. After one breaks the power of grasping, thoughts still arise, but after breaking the power of thoughts through seeing one's underlying true nature, grasping is finished.

10   Guru-Disciple behaviour

Just as an old man must do many things and offer many presents in order to win a beautiful young girl who has many attractive features, so traditionally the disciple must do many things in order to please the Guru who is the site of all good qualities. And the Guru will always act as if he is not pleased or satisfied. For the very stupidest disciples he will act as if he is never satisfied and always oppress them in the manner of a herdsman with his cattle.

11   Guru and faith

The 'outer' object is pure and devoid of inherent self nature. The 'inner' subject is also pure. Resting in the middle point, your awareness will become pure by not relying on artificial interpretation. This is the central teaching of Padmasambhava in the LE'U DUN MA. However you must have faith in the Guru otherwise you could recite these verses for 100,000 years and get no result. Doubts are very dangerous. The Guru may be poor or stupid while other people may be very rich but the Guru has the great treasure of the Dharmadhātu and Sambhogakāya. The rich man cannot save you, but the Guru can and you can gain enlightenment. Even if you become rich yourself that cannot save you. You have to think, *"This world is a very difficult place so I must get free from it and only the Guru can save me."*

Some Tibetans say that Padmasambhava knows more than the present-time Gurus so he is more important but this is not so because we can easily see the Guru but not Padmasambhava. If we have faith that the Guru is not different from Padmasambhava and that he will come to save us, then we get result. Also Padmasambhava, without faith, is a very ordinary man with many wives. Faith is the most important. Dudjom Rinpoche is a very high representative of Padmasambhava. Who you believe much is your root Guru.

If someone is known to be a Terton treasure revealer then we would ask them, *"Do you have La-Grub?"*, *"Do you have Dzogchen?"*, *"Do you have Thugs-Grub?"*. If all three kinds of texts are present in their treasure, then this Terton is Terchen (*gTer-Chen*), a great treasure revealer. If only two of them, then they are a Tertring (*gTer-'Bring*), an ordinary Terton.

Gya-Shang-Trom, a cow-herder found a terma (*gTer-Ma*) under a rock. He showed it to his uncle, Shang-Bo, who became his sponsor (*Chos-bDag*). Shang-Bo threw it in water but it returned. Then he put it on a fire but it was not damaged. Then he put it in a clay pot but it was shining and broke the pot open. One day Gya-Shang-Trom was sleeping and he dreamed that cow-herding girls were dancing around him and a man with a big hat came and beat him. When he woke up he could read and write and later he wrote three large volumes. Then when he was old he had cow-herder disciples. They could not read or study so for seven days he did phowa (*'Pho-Ba*) practice and sent them all to Nirvana and then he died. Three years later his uncle died.

12   Story about devotion

Once upon a time there was a great and famous Guru who had many disciples. Students came from all over to study with him and they would stay for months or years and then leave to practise in caves or become teachers themselves. However this teacher had one student who never seemed to make any progress. He always sat at the front and gazed attentively and devotedly at the teacher. He heard every teaching; he heard it again and again, but he seemed to understand nothing.

After many years the teacher decided he could not help him and asked him to leave. However the disciple exhibited such despair and hopelessness at the thought of leaving that the Guru decided to try one last practice.

He gave his student a recitation mala made of large rudraksha beads and told him that he must go into a strict closed retreat. He was only to do one simple practice – which was to recite the mantra which said, *"Hung. All hail the horn on my head!"*

Years passed and many new students came and people stopped talking of the student who was in retreat. The Guru was getting old and suddenly became very sick. Doctors were called; they tried many medicines but nothing helped. His close students tried many practices but these made no difference. It was clear that the Guru was going to die. A message was sent out to all his students that they should gather to see the teacher for one last time.

Someone remembered the student in his isolated cave and sent him a message. When he heard of his teacher's condition he ran as fast as he could over the high mountain passes. He looked crazy when he arrived, his tattered clothes falling about him. He had wild eyes, a long beard and a mountain of tangled hair piled on top of his head. When he came in front of his teacher he made many rapid full-length prostrations and as he did this his hair unfurled and fell about him revealing a huge horn that had grown on the top of his head. When he bowed in front of his teacher his teacher touched the horn and immediately the teacher's health started to return.

Devotion is the heart of practice.

13   How to get blessing

You must strive for blessing in the way that a child says, *"Mummy, give me an ice cream!"* and then cries and pesters the mother tugging at her until she gives way. If we really believe, the blessing will come. We must think, *"I really trust you so why do you not give me blessing? Why do you not show me!"*

Firstly, we must gain the intrinsic knowing of all-encompassing space,

Dharmadhātujñāna, otherwise the other four are only names. Whoever gets this wisdom of all-encompassing space, Dharmadhātujñāna, automatically gets the other four. The mirror-like wisdom which shows all things clearly, arises with the purification of anger. The wisdom of evenness which, being without bias or preference, shows all things to be equal, arises with the purification of pride. The wisdom of discernment which shows all the details of whatever is occurring, both sins and virtues, arises with the purification of desire. The wisdom of full accomplishment which displays all methods with full power to act, arises with the purification of jealousy.

The wisdom of all-encompassing space has full power; like the sun shining above a mountain its light goes in all directions. But if the sun is shining on one side of the mountain only then its power is limited. Similarly each of the other four wisdoms can only perform particular functions.

With the arising of these wisdoms the afflictions vanish. These wisdoms are not removed from life, they do not block responsiveness but effortlessly provide many effective ways of relating. For example, if you drink cold water when you are hot you will become hot again very quickly, but if you drink hot tea it has a refreshing effect and will cool you down for much longer. In the sphere of the Dharmadhātu there are no relative positions. What do we find there? Its natural inhabitant is Dharmatā, the actuality which never changes or does anything. This is similar to the sky, which is always the same. From Dharmadhātu comes Dharmakāya. Dharmadhātu is like a place. Dharmatā is its nature. Dharmakāya is its form or presence there.

It is vital to experience the Dharmadhātu so that when you die and go unconscious you recognise the Dharmakāya and so do not go the wrong way. Then you will gain the Sambhogakāya and the Nirmanakāya. Without the Sambhogakāya the Nirmanakāya cannot arise. It cannot appear straight from the Dharmakāya.

14 Vows

Why do we take vows? In the Hinayana system vows are like an object made of clay: if they are broken they cannot be repaired. Mahayana vows are like copper: if they are broken then they can be repaired a bit. Vajrayana vows are like gold: if they are broken there is no harm to the gold.

Dam-Tshig, or samaya, or solemn promises, are made in order to gain enlightenment, which means recognising one's own original nature. In Dzogchen the vow is the original nature since the practice is non-dual. The vow is Ngo-Bo, our natural situation or Rang-bZhin, our natural quality. Abiding in one's own situation is the fulfilment of all vows. A woman makes vows at marriage to always stay with her husband and serve him – this covers all her later activities of cooking, raising children and so on. Similarly all offerings and practices are part of the vow, for the vow is to see and abide in our original situation.

15   Full faith

Relaxing and opening to and within the natural clarity of our mind, object vanishes and subject vanishes. The first thought is our present thought, it is the only thought. For example, if a thought arises such as, 'I must do this' then do not continue it. Leave it as it is. It needs no completion. Do not try to stop it or develop it. Don't examine it or get involved. If it is left alone it will go free in its own place.

The ocean always has waves. In the mind there are always thoughts. It is the emptiness of the ocean that allows the waves to move. They stop moving when they reach the beach. In the same way the mind's nature is open like the sky. Don't make a limit, don't block the movement. It is not possible to hold the mind still, to keep it in one place, for it is always moving. If you try to hold your mind you are grasping at a memory, for the thought or feeling or experience has already gone. That memory is a different thought from the one which it is 'remembering' and 'it' has to be put there again and again. Each repetition is different; no moment is exactly the same as any other. It is not possible to hold the sky, for the sky itself is infinite and ungraspable and its contents, the clouds and the wind and so on, are always changing. Likewise, mind is open and empty. It is not possible to fix it in its own place. Just leave it in its own place which is where it always is and then thoughts go free. By following thoughts more thought is stimulated and so it never ceases.

To awaken to this you need full faith in your Guru and Padmasambhava. We pray, "You must do all that is necessary for me. I fully open to you. I want to be like you. You must give me knowledge of my own *nature."* Pray slowly with understanding of the words and with the wish to gain wisdom and be free of the constraint of thoughts. Padmasambhava is the actual Buddha. He is not different from the Buddha and has the same power, qualities and so on. Therefore he is called Orgyen Sangye Nyipa (*O-rGyan Sangs-rGyas gNyis-Pa*), the second Buddha who comes from Orgyan. Some old texts refer to him as Sangye Mi Nyipa (*Sangs-rGyas Mi-gNyis-Pa*), that is, not different (*gNyis-Su-Med*), the one who is not different from the Buddha.

16 The black and white stones

Geshe Potowa (*dGe-Shes Po-To-Ba*) used to practise meditation with a pile of white stones and a pile of black stones in front of him. He would pick up a white stone if he had good thoughts, and a black stone if he had bad thoughts. At first he only had one white stone and many black stones. After six months they were of equal amounts. After two years he had no black stones at all.

He asked Atisha if this was enough. Atisha told him that he should continue practising till there were no stones at all; he was to free himself from the perception of duality, of distinguishing between good and bad. Atisha said, *"Now you have stopped doing sins but not stopped karma from the past. You must practise śūnyatā, emptiness."* And he taught him this. Firstly he showed him that all objects are empty and he got the result. Then he showed him that the subject is empty and with this he finished all his sins and obscurations. Atisha said to him, *"Now even if we bind you with chains and weights, and throw you in hell, you would not stay there."*

Stopping sins is one part of practice but you must get śūnyatā to really stop sins and gain enlightenment. You will only really understand karma when you get śūnyatā. When we do sins we create bad karma. This arises due to the afflictions, whose root is ignorance. Ignorance is darkness from which comes desire, pride and so on. When you know śūnyatā then wisdom shines forth and all sins stop. With śūnyatā you see that the subject is impermanent and so cut egoism.

17 Purifying our bad actions

The root of all trouble is ignorance. It is the source of egoism and due to it, desire, anger and so on arise. It is the sole root and it is the opposite of awareness, intrinsic knowing, and wise discernment. Whether I become a Buddha or whether I go to hell, awareness never changes. It is always clear, always good, never mixed. Stupid ignorance covers that wisdom for us like a pot placed over a lamp. It is necessary to break the pot so that the permanent light shines forth.

At the early stages of practice we need to say, *"forgive me."* We need someone to clean us; this is the first factor of purification. We need to say, *"Excuse me"* to the man who has the power to purify our sins. This is Vajrasattva. All the Buddhas have power to help, so why is Vajrasattva employed especially for purifying our sins? All students while training have some main idea, like medicine or engineering. Similarly when the great Bodhisattvas were training they thought of different ways to help beings. At that time Vajrasattva made a firm intention to free all beings from their sins.

Why do we say, *"Excuse me"*? This is how we acknowledge that we have done bad things; this is the second factor of purification. We know that these actions were sins, for example stealing. This causes trouble to others and it means that I also will get trouble. You must think that you are dying from sin as if you had taken poison. With this understanding you develop great fear; this is the third factor of purification.

Then you must promise and firmly decide that in future you will never do it again. This vow or promise is the fourth factor of purification.

With these four factors we separate our mind from our habit of selfish egoism. Now we can appreciate how these habits appear to be 'me' and we also see that they are not actually 'me'. When we identify with our assumptions and habits they seem to be 'us'. Yet when we stand apart from them we see that they are not 'us'. This mixing or confusion is what we ask Vajrasattva to wash out of us.

A student of Dudjom Rinpoche's first incarnation was a butcher and while he was washing the stomach of dead animals he believed that all sins were being washed out. After practising this he stayed in a cave in retreat and then flew in the sky. It is also said that when he went for teaching he was taught that everything was illusion, gyuma (*sGyu-Ma*), but he heard it as everything was sausages made with intestines, gyuma (rGyu-Ma). So by one-pointed attention to his daily practice of making sausages, he became enlightened!

18   The ground

From the ground (gZhi) the delusory appearances ('Khrul-sNang) of subject and object arise. They are confusing because under their power we believe that something is the case when it is not. Then, becoming at home in that confusion, it seems to be just how things are and we take it to be clarifying rather than confusing. By the interplay of subject and object the ground itself is not recognised. When the ground is recognised their power ends. They are not different from the ground.

For example, if our ground nature is Room 8 in a building, confusion ('Khrul-Pa) is to not like Room 8. Due to this we cannot really see Room 8 as it is but only in terms of our prejudice. Truly seeing Room 8 as it is, we awaken from bewilderment and in that liberation we see that confusion, our belief about Room 8, was not different from the ground, the open spacious potential which is the actuality of Room 8. Staying in Room 8 is the ground, not liking Room 8 and so daydreaming that you're somewhere else, is confusion. But actually Room 8 is okay in itself so we must wake up on Room 8 itself as it is. Thus confusion is non-dual with the ground. It is naturally arising, a natural form, empty of inherent self-nature. What gives confusion its power is our own belief in it.

By taking confusion to be an obstacle, to be something other than the ground which has to be removed, one has not really shifted from the position of believing that the confusion is truly existing in itself. By recognising the activity of sleep-like confusion we wake up *on the basis of the ground*. Then confusion is self-liberating; it is neither to be adhered to nor avoided.

For example, if a Chinese child was adopted by European parents and raised in Europe the child would one day awaken to the fact that these people were not her biological parents. On the basis of this she becomes what she has always been, Chinese. Or, another example, on the basis of living in a country where there are many snakes, while walking outside in the dark night, you see a rope and think it is a snake, and then many fears arise. If you then take out your torch and focus it at the snake, then on the basis of seeing that it is in fact a rope, you awaken from these fears.

From the ground comes the bewilderment therefore bewilderment must wake up, or dissolve itself, or vanish *on* the ground. In sleep you could wake up from unconsciousness inside a dream but this is still a form of unconsciousness and you are still confused. It is necessary to wake up *on* consciousness free of all unconsciousness, that is, on awareness. A prince becomes a king *on* his parents, that is to say, it is on the basis of having royal parents that the prince is entitled to be king. If a thief steals money he *has* money but the situation is unstable because the money does not really belong to him. But if a man inherits money from his father, this money is really his on the basis of his father. It is *on* the fact of his father being his father that he has the money. It is *on* the fact of our source, our ground, that we awaken. What is truly ours arises on, and from, and in, the ground. It is ours, it is us, but not as a personal, private or separate possession.

It is not about developing something new. For fundamental awakening, all the rich creativity of your imagination is not required. Imagining new possibilities and developing new technologies will not lead to enlightenment. Enlightenment is the awakening of the potentiality of the ground. It is not something new. It can't be purchased, or made. It is always present as the ground of every experience.

19   Dharmatā

The knower, awareness itself, our own presence, does not make or do anything but remains true to its own nature without being artificial. Even great scholars are not able to construct it. When we become distracted we can go under the power of various tendencies such as a helpless drifting (*'Bying-Ba*) and sinking (*'Thibs-Pa*). With drifting (*'Bying-Ba*), like a tired swimmer who has no energy left but is kept going by the force of the waves, the meditator has no energy to maintain clarity and direction and is moved hither and thither by the waves of thoughts, feelings and so on. With sinking (*'Thibs-Pa*), the overpowering forces get stronger, increasing one's helpless confusion. Yet the mind itself is never trapped in the prison of these experiences, therefore stay present on the knower itself and whatever is arising will go free by itself without causing help or harm.

Dharmatā is infinite like the sky. It is the actuality of our true nature. It is our ground and so is described as the mother. Our ordinary mind that has been mixed with confusion needs to recognise the mother and to join with it again like a child returning home. If this is experienced, we will not go under the power of lazy distraction and will not get lost and will abide in the house of the Dharmadhātu. If you do this you will have full awareness and be integrated with the Dharmadhātu and so be able to work continuously for the benefit of others.

We must understand Dharmatā or actuality, clearly. It is raw and naked (rJen-Pa), without secrets, our direct original nature. It is emptiness, śūnyatā, thusness, Tathata, Sugatagarbha, Tathatagarbha, the ground or basis of all the Buddhas. If you understand this then all that can be seen or experienced is immediately and directly known (sNang-Rig). With this there is great clarity inseparable from emptiness (gSal-sTong).

When this is awakened to your body and your world are like a rainbow. If you see śūnyatā directly you will not have any sins or obscuration – when the sun rises all the darkness and cold immediately clears. Flesh, blood, and bone are ended and the light body is gained ('Ja-'Od Thig-Le'i-Khams).

This term also indicates that when we understand Dharmatā, spheres of light (Thig-Le) are seen in front of our eyes. At first they are black and white, and then four or five come one after another in a row, or like a lotus petal, or move, going away and coming towards the eye.

This term also indicates that all that is in the Dharmadhātu is in the form of spheres of light. This is radiance without substance; appearance, clarity and awareness inseparable from emptiness. With the wisdom of all-encompassing awareness the other four are automatically present for they are its qualities – just as when one walks in the sunlight one's shadow is automatically immediately there.

From this rainbow-light the symbols of the meditation deities manifest, for example vajra and bell for Dorje Dragpo Tsal and a vajra for Dorje Zhonu, and one manifests full awakening with the five kāya modes of enlightened being, and the five jñāna wisdoms. In this way we gain or awaken to the full primordially pure original śūnyatā nature.

20   Our true nature

Our true nature (*Ngo-Bo*), is unborn depth. It is awareness inseparable from space and depth (*dhātu*) which is emptiness. It is essential to focus on this, your own nature. This is the infinite space of awareness in your own heart where awareness emerges as a point. This is the heart point (*sNying-Thig*) – in the heart there is one empty point which is the form of emptiness, of śūnyatā. This is the site of awareness. If it is blocked by blood then one dies.

From this point, natural clarity (*Rang-bZhin*), the inherent quality of our true nature, radiates as a sphere of five colours within the heart. With this our energy or compassion (*Thugs-rJe*) emerges as the display of the activities of the components or skandhas, potentials or dhātus, and so on, as a light form in a world of light forms. Our awareness (*vidya*) is simply knowing, pure knowing. *Ngo-Bo*, *Rang-bZhin* and *Thugs-rJe* are its modes of knowing, its non-dual 'object' (*dhātu*) and all that appears in the space of dhātu.

Liberation lies in recognising and keeping to our true nature (*Ngo-Bo*), and not getting seduced by the magnificence of self-display (*Rang-bZhin*). As long as there is any resting on or in what arises, there is no security. The secure place of Vajradhara (*rDo-rJe 'Chang-Gi-bTsan-Sa*) is Dharmadhātu. This is the direct experience or knowing of the infinite openness of one's being. All relative identities, whether as hell-being or as heruka, are the manifesting of dependent co-origination (*rTen-Ching Brel-Bar 'Byung-Ba*) and so are not ultimate. They are not the natural unchanging situation. If our true nature (*Ngo-Bo*) is directly experienced, not one atom of arising need be rejected because then one sees that everything is non-dual radiance.

But if this is not realised then there is grasping at entities and then karma is produced and one finds oneself wandering in the six realms. One's behaviour becomes artificial and full of contrivance (*bCos-bCas bZo-Byed*). Interfering with whatever is occurring, the mind is kept busy and is unable to rest in its own place (*Rang-Sar Ma-bZhag-Pa*). Thus due to reification and dualistic vision one experiences fixation and polarisation, involvement of subject and object, and karmic activity.

21   Atiyoga and Adiyoga

The great perfection or completion, Dzogpachenpo (*rDzogs-Pa Chen-Po*), is also known as Atiyoga or Adiyoga. Ati means topmost, the very highest. Adi means primordial, prime, before mind became false. This teaching appears in three sections or groups. There is the mind section (*Sems-sDe*). This points out that everything is the mind, mind does everything, there is nothing else. Everything is emptiness but it is mind that gives rise to everything. Even emptiness, śūnyatā, is known by mind. The space section (*kLong-dDe*) points out that everything is śūnyatā, infinite depth and expanse. *kLong* is the vastness in which everything is emptiness. It is infinite space itself. The instruction section (*Man-Ngag-sDe*) offers the teachings of the mind and space sections in a form that can be practised.

22   Vairocana and Sri Sinha

Vairocana had received many teachings from Sri Sinha but still he was not satisfied so Sri Sinha said,

ཆོས་ཀྱི་དབྱིངས་ལ་ཟད་མེད་གྱུང་།

དེ་བཞིན་ཉིད་ཀྱི་གཅིག་ཤེས་ན།

མ་ལུས་དེ་ལ་ཡོངས་སུ་རྫོགས།

དེ་ལས་ཡོད་ན་ སེ་ཧ་གན།

"Although infinite hospitality is never exhausted,
if you know the true nature of just one thing
then you will have complete knowledge of all.
I, Sri Sinha promise this."

Sri Sinha is saying to Vairocana: you are not satisfied but the Dharmadhātu never finishes so how will you gain full knowledge? How can you possibly keep track of every teaching? But if you know the nature of just one thing, if you see its actuality, its thusness, it's Tathata directly, then that is enough. I promise that there is nothing more than this. This points to the fact that the result naturally comes out, it is naturally revealed within (*'Bras-Bu Rang-Chas-Su sTon-Pa*). There is no end to looking if you look in the wrong place. Don't look at the object. Don't look at the current content of the subject. Look at the looker. By being the looker enter the situation of non-dual presence and then everything is clear.

23   C.R. Lama on his throne

Mindfulness is the middle way. To be mindful is to be present, not going to the left or right, not leaping forward and not falling back. For example, when I was young and living in my monastery I sat on a throne like the other high lamas although I did not know very much at that time. At the end of the public rituals, sponsors and other people would come forward to present ceremonial scarves and offerings. When I was presented with a scarf I had to lean forward and drape it around the sponsor's neck. However not every sponsor offered me a scarf. I had to be ready to bend forward if one was offered and to sit still in equanimity if one was not offered. If I leaned forward when one was not offered or sat still when one was offered, my teacher who was sitting beside me, would hit me on the back of the head. Thus I was trained in mindfulness.

24   The King tries to help his people

It is very important for human beings not to waste their life in laziness. However it is also important not to waste your life in unhelpful or unproductive activity. For example, when King Srongtsen Gampo first converted to Buddhism he became very inspired by the beautiful vision of love and compassion that he learned about. He looked around him at his people and saw how different they each were. Some were sick and some were healthy. Some were beautiful and some were ugly. Some were rich and some were poor. He realised that even as a great king he could not alter people's health or beauty by a law, however he could change their financial circumstances. So he published an edict declaring that at the end of the month all the wealth of the country was to be gathered together.

A great mountain of possessions was created and this was then redistributed fairly amongst all the people of Tibet. *"Ah"*, he thought, *"now my people should be happy."* However after a year he noticed that again some people were rich and some people were poor so he arranged another redistribution. At the end of that year, again he saw that some were rich and some were poor. This awakened in him a direct understanding of the power of karma. What arises manifests the energy and consequence of actions performed long before. No matter how he tried to impose justice, the individual patterns of people's karma caused them to experience precisely their own share of the world.

If we want to help people the key focus has to be on helping them to cut the root of duality for it is this root which generates all the many karmic tendencies and impulses. Trying to alter the patterns of behaviour from outside is doomed to failure. That is why we must recognise and work with circumstances and the precise capacity of different individuals.

25   Dorje and Bell

The Tibetan word for a small bell is *Dril-Bu*; *Dril* means sound. Different kinds of drilbu are described in tantras such as the Hevajra tantra, the Kalachakra tantra, the Vajrakilaya tantra and so on and they are also mentioned in Kriyayoga tantras. The mansion or palace of Kalachakra is shaped like a bell.

Instructions for building stupas include the making of a chain of bells, drilbu, around the stupa and the consecration ceremony for the stupa also makes reference to these drilbu.

Monasteries have a bell to waken the monks and another big bell is used during invitations and blessings in the rituals. There are also bells used as wind chimes to remind people of the thirty-seven Bodhisattva practices. Some sutras describe how a bell was tied on an elephant's trunk and then the person whom the elephant touched with its trunk was recognised as a king.

Such bells did not have symbols on them unlike the Tibetan drilbu bells which have OM A HUNG cast inside them at the top, in the area called the 'drilbu's womb'. Some drilbus, like mine, have no images cast inside them and these are called *Myangs-'Das Dril-Bu*, paranirvana drilbus. They were cast when Shakyamuni Buddha died and so were called 'sadness bells'. One hundred and eight such bells were made and many of them, including mine, came to Tibet with the Bodhisattva Atiśa Dīpaṃkara Śrījñāna. They were made in different sizes. Mine has a silver head, as do all the original bells. Later copies were made and their heads are of mixed metals.

Drilbus are classified according to shape, for example with five or nine prongs, or according to the country where they were made, or according to the ornamentation on the 'skirts'.

Shapes include those of Uddiyana, Nalanda and Bodhgaya. There is a Nepalese style which differs from that in other countries. In Upper Tibet and Tsang they use a bell which is sometimes wrongly called a Tashilhunpo drilbu since this shape is used in other monasteries also, such as in Khordong monastery. Other bells are the Tsa-dril, Hor-dril, Shing-dril [of the Shan dynasty], Chang-dril, Tsok-dril, Nyarong-dril, Derge-dril, Den-dril, Lhasa-dril, Shigatse-dril, Kalimpong-dril, Bir-dril, Clementown-dril, Nepali-dril, Rajpur-dril, Byalakuppe-dril and so on.

Gold, silver, lead, copper, tin, bronze and iron are the metals used for making dorjes and drilbu as well as alloys such as tung, an alloy similar to pewter which is white in colour and less valuable than silver. Jang (lJang) is a pure metal and should it get broken when it is old, the inside metal has the colour of jade. Jang (lJang) is also an area[1] where jade comes from. Large bells, cymbals, long-life vases, bumpas and butterlamps can also be made of this metal and some of the bumpas have fingerprints visible on the metal.

Bells make different sounds according to the proportions of the various metals used. If there is a lot of gold, the bell sounds HUNG HUNG HUNG. If there is a lot of silver, the bell sounds SHUNG SHUNG SHUNG. If there is a lot of tung white metal, the bell sounds CHAG, CHAG, CHAG. In the Indian system eight metals were used and the proportions varied.

Regarding their shape, the dorje and the drilbu have the same number of prongs. Padmasambhava's termas describe nine-pronged ones and these are used only in the Nyingma practices.

The dorje is a symbol of strength. There is an account of one yogi who died and attained the vajra body, with all his finger joints being separate vajras and his forearms like the vajra of Indra, which is a different shape from the Tibetan vajra. Vajra is something that is very strong and cannot be destroyed. When deities hold a vajra it is a symbol of victory and subduing.

Some tantras refer to a dorje with a hundred prongs, (rDo-rJe rTse-brGya-Pa) and there are also dorjes with four and with five prongs. The prongs pointing up represent the male dhyani Buddhas and the prongs pointing down represent the female dhyani Buddhas. The central prong represents Vairocana. To the East is Vajrasattva, the South is Ratnasambhava, to the West is Amitabha and to the North is Amoghasiddhi.

On the drilbu, below the figure on the shaft and starting under the deity's nose, that is to say, in the East, there are five letters, ཉཾ ལཾ མཾ པཾ ཏཾ Mum Lam Mam Pam Tam. These are symbols for the five female dhyani Buddhas and these letters are the equivalent of the five lower prongs on the dorje. Sometimes there are eight letters, but this is not correct. If there are eight letters, these are ཏཾ མཾ ལཾ པཾ མཾ ཙཾ པཾ བྷྲཾ Tam Mam Lam Pam Mam Tsum Pam Bhrum. These eight letters would correspond to the eight lotus petals around the 'waist' of the dorje, which signify the eight Bodhisattvas and their eight consorts.

Regarding the ornamentation of the drilbu, the eight water-monster (Chu-Srin) heads, represent the eight consciousnesses. The long jeweled garlands hanging from their mouths are a symbol of the purification of the obscurations, klesas and also represent the decorations on the outer walls of the mandala. The four drops at the end of tassels signify the 'four immeasurables', love, compassion, joy and equanimity.

Between the water-monsters' faces there may be ornaments symbolising the eight great Bodhisattvas. The sequence starts from the East, below the deity's nose. It may be the eight auspicious ornaments which can vary and may include a wheel or moon, a jewel, a lotus, a knife, crossed vajras, a single vajra, flowers and other additional things. These ornaments are a symbol for the Rupakāya and the eight upper letters are a symbol of the Dharmakāya.

Around the rim at the base of the bell, enclosed within two rows of pearls, is a ring of upright vajras, forming a vajra fence or protective circle (Srung-'Khor).

Around the top of the bell, between two rings of pearls, there is a ring of horizontal vajras, a protective circle representing the boundary of samsara and nirvana and the eight or sixteen emptinesses.

Inside the bell, the upper part of the bell represents Dharmakāya and the lower part represents Rupakāya, that is, the Sambhogakāya and the Nirmanakāya.

The bell does not vary according to the mandala practice, nor to the tantra nor to the school, however in general we Nyingmapa use a five-pronged dorje and drilbu for peaceful practices and a nine-pronged dorje and drilbu for wrathful practices.

At the base of the upper handle of a five-pointed drilbu there can be a a long-life vase (*Tshe-Bum*) with jewels. A nine-pronged drilbu will not have such a long-life vase but instead will have an open ring through which you can put your finger when doing certain practices, such as wrathful dances.

Regarding the use of the dorje and bell, other than when we are reciting mantras, we should hold the dorje and bell all the time, keeping the dorje upright, with the prongs representing the male Dhyani Buddhas on top. Since there is no way by looking to tell the difference between the top and the bottom of the dorje, we need to do something to help us, such as marking the dorje at the time of initiation or at its conse-cration. Especially when doing Vajrasattva practice we should hold the vajra, dorje, because Vajrasattva belongs to the vajra family. At other times, according to Jangter and Khordong practice, we hold the dorje at our chest, using the thumb and three middle fingers of our right hand and with our left hand holding the bell at our left knee. When we are saying a prayer, we can hold the dorje and bell, or if we do not have them, simply hold our hands in the prayer mudra.

When we lay them down, the Jangter system is to place the drilbu facing east towards you, with the dorje laid across in front of it, not touching. The upper part of the dorje should be on your left, the lower part on your right. When picking them up, pick them both up at the same time.

NOTES

[1] The Naxi region of Yunnan province.

11

Khordong Monastery

Khordong Monastery is situated in East Tibet, in Trehor Province, sNyi-Yul District near the village of Deva. The Deva family were the first to come to that area and, until the 1960's, were the most important house and the largest landowners. The village took its name from that family.

The monastery is known both as Khordong Gompa (*'Khor-gDong dGon-Pa*) and as Khangdong Gompa (*Khang-gDong dGon-Pa*). The monastery was constructed in about 1725 AD by Khamtrul Sherab Membar (*Khams-sPrul Shes-Rab Me-'Bar*) who was born in 1680 AD in the iron-snake (*lCags-sBrul*) year of the 11th *Rab-'Byung* cycle. He was born in the house of Deva Tshang.

Up until the 1950's in Golok and Sertag areas, the people elected their chief (*dPon-Po*) and their officers and 'kings'. The central government had no soldiers there and the people paid no tax to them. Between these two areas lies Trehor Nyi Khog and on their border area is Deva village.

According to the tradition, one hundred generations after the Deva family first built their house there, the head of the house was called Ngagnag Namchag Membar (*sNgags-Nag gNam-lCags Me-'Bar*). His name was Namchag Membar (*gNam-lCags Me-'Bar*) and, as he was a powerful and dangerous tantric yogi, he was given the title, Ngagnag (*sNgags-Nag*), 'Black Mantra'. He was very famous because if he became angry he would bring down rain and hail and thunderbolts against his enemies. It is said that throughout the generations the family had been committed to tantric practice.

Namchag Membar had gained his meditation power (*siddhi*) by completing the Black God Phurpa practice of the Northern Treasure (*Byang-gTer Phur-Pa Lha-Nag*). His young son had a very sharp mind and so he called him Sherab (*Shes-Rab*), 'Wise Discernment'. Sherab wanted to know about the teachings of his father's Jangter (*Byang-gTer*) lineage. When he heard that the main monastery was called Dorje Drag (*rDo-rJe Brag*), he wanted to go there even though it was in Central Tibet. At Dorje Drag he received many initiations and teachings. He became a disciple of Rigdzin Pema Trinle (*Rig-'Dzin Pad-Ma 'Phrin-Las*), the fourth Rigdzin Chenpo (*Rig-'Dzin Chen-Po*) and reincarnation of Rigdzin Godem (*Rig-'Dzin rGod-lDem*) and received from him all the initiations and full lineage transmission of Jangter. In return he gave Pema Trinle the East Tibetan lineages of Ratna Lingpa (*Ratna gLing-Pa*), the Khongsal Nyingthig Terchö (*Khong-gSal sNying-Thig gTer-Chos*) and the direct kama (*bKa'-Ma*) lineage. He was also a dharma brother of Pema Trinle as they received initiation together from the fifth Dalai Lama, Ngawang Lobzang Gyamtso (*Ngag-dBang bLo-bZang rGya mTsho*), also known as Zilnon Dragtsal Dorje (*Zil-gNon Drag-rTsal rDo-rJe*).

The origins of the Byang-gTer Lineage

In the eighth century AD the Indian Mahapandita Śantarakshita, Mahacharya Mahasiddha Padmasambhava of Uddiyana and the Tibetan King Trisrong Detsen (*Khri-Srong lDe'u-bTsan*) built Samye (*bSam-Yas*) Monastery. Padmasambhava gave many tantric initiations there and at Samye Chimphu (*bSam-Yas mChims-Phu*) to those who were known as the Thugse Lobu Bugu (*Thugs-Sras sLob-Bu Bu-dGu*), the nine intimate disciples and to the group known as the Lechen Dagpai Khornga (*Las-Can Dag-Pa'i 'Khor-lNga*), the fortunate circle of five and to the Jebang Nyernga (*rJe-'Bangs Nyer-lNga*), the twenty-five disciples comprising the king and his subjects. All these groupings of disciples include Nanam Dorje Dudjom (*sNa-Nam rDo-rJe bDud-'Joms*), King Trisrong Detsen, Khandro Yeshe Tsogyal (*mKha'-'Gro Ye-Shes mTsho-rGyal*), Lhasre Mutri Tsenpo (*Lha-Sras Mu-Tri bTsan-Po*) and Gelong Namkhai Nyingpo (*dGe-sLong Nam-mKha'i sNying-Po*).

Moreover there was the grouping known as Thugse Dagpa Sum (*Thugs-Sras Dag-Pa gSum*), comprising King Trisrong Detsen, Nanam Dorje Dudjom and Yeshe Tsogyal. When Nanam Dorje Dudjom received the initiation for the Eight Great Practices (*sGrub-Chen bKa'-brGyud*) his flower fell in the northern (*Byang*) segment of the mandala and so his meditation deity was Dorje Phurba (*rDo-rJe Phur-Pa*).

Centuries later Nanam Dorje Dudjom incarnated as Rigdzin Gokyi Demtruchen (*Rig-'Dzin rGod-Kyi lDem-sPru-Can*). His birth name was Ngodrub Gyaltsan (*dNgos-sGrub rGyal-mTshan*) but he was called 'Vulture Feather' since first three and then two further vulture feathers grew out of the top of his head. He went to Zang-Zang Lha-Brag and took out the treasure known as Sedrom Mugpo (*bSe-sGrom sMug-Po*), the maroon leather casket. This casket contained five compartments: *sNying-mDzod sMug-Po*, the maroon heart treasury, in the centre; *gDung-mDzod dKar-Po*, the white conch treasury, in the east; *gSer-mDzod Ser-Po*, the yellow golden treasury, in the south; *Zangs-mDzod Mar-Po*, the red copper treasury, in the west; *lCags-mDzod lJang-Gu*, the green iron treasury, in the north. The casket contained the CHIDRUB DROWA KUNDROL (*sPyi-sGRUB sGRO-BA KUN-GROL*), the outer practice of Chenresi; NANGDRUB RIGDZIN DUNGDRUB (*sNANG-sGRUB RIG-'DZIN gDUNG-sGRUB*), the inner practice of Padmasambhava; SANGDRUB DORJE DRAGPO TSAL THINGKA (*gSANG-sGRUB rDO-rJE DRAG-PO-rTSAL mTHING-KHA*), the secret practice of the wrathful blue Dorje Dragpo Tsal; YANGSANG GONGPA ZANGTHAL (*YANG-gSANG dGONGS-PA ZANG-THAL*), secret dzogchen teaching; KABGYE DRAGPO RANJUNG RANGSHAR (*bKA'-brGYAD DRAG-PO RANG-BYUNG RANG-SHAR*), the eight great wrathful deity practices; PHURBA LHANAG DRILDRUB (*PHUR-PA LHA-NAG DRIL-GRUB*), the intense practice of the Black God Nail. All these practices have large and small branches and associated practices and all this together is known as Jangter, the Northern Treasures.

The principal lineage holders of the Byang-gTer are the incarnations of Rigdzin Godem. They each have the title of Rigdzin Chenpo, great bearer of awareness. The second Rigdzin Chenpo, Legden Dudjom Dorje (*Legs-dDan bDud-'Joms rDo-rJe*) was born at Ngari Lobo (*mNga'-Ris gLo-Bo*). The third incarnation was Rigdzin Ngagi Wangpo (*Rig-'Dzin Ngag-Gi dBang-Po*) who was born at Chang Nam-Re. The fourth incarnation was Lobzang Pema Thrinle (*bLo-bZang Padma 'Phrin-Las*) who was born at Namseling (*rNam Sres-gLing*) in Monkhar

(*Mon-mKhar*). He developed Dorje Drag monastery. The fifth incarnation was Kalzang Pema Wangchug (*bsKal-bZang Padma dBang-Phyug*). The sixth incarnation was Khamsum Zilnon Kunzang Gyurme Lhundrub Dorje (*Khams-gSum Zil-gNon Kun-bZang 'Gyur-Med Lhun-Grub rDo-rJe*), who was born at Tachienlu as the son of the local king, Chagla Gyalpo (*lCags-La rGyal-Po*). The seventh incarnation was Ngawang Jampal Mingyur Lhundrub Dorje (*Ngag-dBang 'Jam-dPal Mi-'Gyur Lhun-Grub rDo-rJe*) who was born in the same house as Pema Thrinle. The eighth incarnation was Kalzang Pema Wangyal Dudul Dorje (*sKal-bZang Padma dBang-rGyal bDud-'Dul rDo-rJe*). The ninth incarnation was Thubten Chöwang Nyamnyid Dorje (*Thub-bsTan Chos-dBang mNyam-Nyid rDo-rJe*) who was born in Lhasa. The tenth and current incarnation, Thubten Jigme Namdrol Gyamtso (*Thub-bsTan 'Jig-Med rNam-Grol rGya-mTsho*), was born in Lhasa at Banasho Lha Kyi.

The fourth Rig-'Dzin Chen-Po was Pema Trinle, the disciple and attendant (*Zhabs-Drung*) of the fifth Dalai Lama, Ngawang Lobzang Gyamtso. The fifth Dalai Lama's guru was the third Rigdzin Chenpo, Rigdzin Ngagi Wangpo and he took his own first name, Ngawang (*Ngag-dBang*), from his guru's name. Lobzang (*bLo-bZang*) comes from his first incarnation's name and Gyamtso (*rGya-mTsho*) is a general title applied to all Dalai Lamas.

The fifth Dalai Lama gave Padma Pema Trinle his name in the following way. From the third Rigdzin Chenpo, he gave Ngawang and from his own name he gave Lobzang. Because Pema Trinle was a great lineage holder of Padmasambhava he also received the name Pema (*Padma*) and because, since the time of Rigdzin Godem, he was the one who did the most to develop the Jangter teaching and practice, he was called Trinle (*'Phrin-Las*), activity.

Pema Trinle had as his disciple Sherab Membar who was extremely learned and had received many initiations and transmissions. Pema Trinle already had thirty-two tulkus (*sPrul-sKu*, incarnation lamas) studying with him when Sherab Membar arrived — but the newcomer proved to be the best at study and so was named Sherab Membar because his knowledge (*Shes-Rab*) was like a blazing fire (*Me-'Bar*). He was also a dharma brother of Pema Trinle since they were both disciples of the fifth Dalai Lama. When Sherab Membar took the full ordination as a monk his name was Jampa Tenpai Gyaltsen (*Byams-Pa bsTan-Pa'i rGyal-mTshan*).

The fifth Dalai Lama instructed Sherab Membar with this prediction, *"You must return to your own house. Nearby there is a mountain where three naga snake gods stay. At that place Nubchen Sangye Yeshe (gNubs-Can Sangs-rGyas Ye-Shes) meditated on Shinje (Yamantaka, gShin-rJe-Shed). It is a place where meditation ripens quickly. Nearby there is a prayer wheel and you should go there and practise diligently. You must build a meditation house there and name it Thubten Evam Sangngag Chokor Namgyal Ling (Thub-bsTan E-Vam gSang-sNgag Chos-'Khor rNam-rGyal gLing)."* The fifth Dalai Lama gave him his working seal and this has come down to me.

Rigdzin Chenpo Pema Trinle gave him a complete set of all the Dorje Drag texts and tsagli (*Tsag-Li*) initiation drawings, totaling twelve boxes in all. He also sent thirteen monks to accompany him as the senior monk. Twelve of the monks each carried one of the boxes while the thirteenth carried the food. At that time Sherab Membar was about forty-six years of age.

When he arrived at his home he began to search for the spot he had been told about. To the north-east of his home was a small spring called Lugyal Zhugmo (*kLu-rGyal Zhug-Mo*) and near it two springs called Ritro Chumig Yela and Ritro Chumig Yonla (*Ri-Khrod Chu-Mig gYas-La gYon-La*). These springs were very small yet they always had water and in winter there was steam on top of the water and small frogs and shrimps lived in it. In the middle of this area he saw a very old house which had fallen down but could find no trace of a prayer wheel.

Sherab Membar stayed there for three months and then he had a dream which showed him where the prayer wheel was. When he went to that spot he could not find it but he decided that he would spend a few days there. Then at night, when it was very quiet, he heard the sound of the wheel turning. Locating it the next day he found that the prayer wheel had been placed under the earth and that it was being turned by the wind blowing on the feathers attached to it. This wheel had been built by Nubchen Sangye Yeshe (*gNubs-Chen Sangs-rGyas Ye-Shes*) at the time of Padmasambhava. The huge prayer-wheel was filled with mantras of Yamantaka. It was turned by the wind through tunnels and in the winter, due to the formation of ice, it could be heard making a grinding sound.

He built a small temple nearby and inside it he placed the thangka scroll paintings of the deities of the eight great practices (*bKa'-brGyad*) with a thangka painted by Pema Trinle at the centre. This practice centre was known by the name given by the fifth Dalai Lama and was commonly known as Khordong monastery.

His thirteen companions built the following branch monasteries:

1. Thubten Evam Sangngag Chökor Zhugjung Ling (*Thub-bsTan E-Vam gSang-sNgags Zhug-'Byung gLing*) also known as Zhugjung Gompa (*Zhug-'Byung dGon-Pa*) was constructed by Jigtral Gyamtso (*'Jigs-Bral rGya-mTsho*) in mDo-Khog.

2. Tagtse (*sTag-rTse*) built by Namdrol Gyamtso (*rNam-Grol rGya-mTsho*) in Nyar-Tri.

3. Zhugchen Gompa (*gZhug-Chen dGon-Pa*) was built by Yeshe Gyamtso (*Ye-Shes rGya-mTsho*) in gZhi-'Khor.

4. Ratrom (*Ra-Krom*) by Nudon Zangpo (*Nus-Don bZang-Po*) in sNyi-sMad.

5. Bala Gompa (*Ba-Lar dGon*) by Kunga Ngedon (*Kun-dGa' Nges-Don*) in Mi-Nyag village.

6. Bane Gompa (*Ba-gNas dGon*) by Yeshe Dorje (*Ye-Shes rDo-rJe*) in Ba Khog village.

7. Do Dorje Drag (*mDo rDo-rJe Brag*) by Namdrol Dorje Zangpo (*rNam-sGrol rDo-rJe bZang-Po*) at Tachienlu. The Dorje Drag Lha-Brang was named after the sixth Rigdzin Chenpo, Khamsum Zilnon (*Rig-'Dzin Chen-Po Khams-gSum Zil-gNon*), who was born in that place and who then went to Dorje Drag monastery in central Tibet.

8. Tribu Gompa (*Tri-Bu dGon*) by Kunga Thegchog Tenpai Gyaltsen (*Kun-dGa' Theg-mChog bsTan-Pai rGyal-mTshan*) at Ba village. He was the highest scholar and greatest meditator and most senior disciple in the circle of Pema Trinle. Sherab Membar, when dying, appointed him to be the senior teacher.

9. Thubten Evam Gatsal (*Thub-bsTan E-Vam dGa'-mTshal*) meditation retreat centre was built by Trinle Lhundrub (*'Phrin-Las Lhun-sGrub*) near Khordong monastery. Meditators there focussed on the preliminary practices (*sNgon-'Gro*), the energy practices (*Phag-Mo Zab-rGyas*) and the nature of the mind (*rDzog-Chen Ka-Dag*) and were renowned for their success in practice.

10. Tsone Gompa (*gTso-gNas dGon*) built by Urgyen Chemchog (*U-rGyan Che-mChog*) in gTso village.

11. Drori Ritro (*'Bro-Ri Ri-Khrod*) hermitage built by Kunga Yeshe (*Kun-dGa' Ye-Shes*) at bSer-Khog.

12. Sotogne (*bSo-Thog gNas*) monastery built by Thogme Zangpo (*Thog-Med bZang-Po*) at gTso village.

13. Drala Gompa (*Gra-Lags dGon*) built by Sherab Gyamtso (*Shes-Rab rGya-mTsho*) at Dza village.

14. Gutsa Gompa (*'Gu-Tsha dGon*) built by Sherab Zangpo in upper Zu village.

15. Nelung Gompa (*sNe-Lung dGon*) built by Sherab Zangpo.

16. Pangle Gompa (*sPang-Le dGon*) built by Sherab Zangpo.

The head monastery of these fifteen centres is Khordong Gompa built by Sherab Membar. At Khordong Gompa there were 108 temples and one very big stupa which took six years to build. It was very costly to build. All the gold and butter and riches of the area were sold to make the stupa. Due to this all the people of the area became poor, their egoism was cut and consequently fighting and squabbling ceased. Sherab Membar received full transmission of all initiations and teachings (*Thob-Yig*) from the fifth Dalai Lama. He gave these in their full form to Khordong Terchen (*'Khor-gDong gTer-Chen*) directly and to Drubgon Tse (*sGrub-mGon Tsheg*) and Tenpa Gyaltsen (*bsTan-Pa rGyal-mTshan*).

Khordong Terchen Nuden Dorje gave the full lineage to his nephew Gonpo Wangyal (*dGon-Po dBang-rGyal*) and to Rigdzin Chomdar (*Rig-'Dzin Chos-mDar*) of Bane Gompa. They both gave full transmission to Tulku Tsorlo (*sPrul-sKu Tshul-Lo*) and Tulku Tsorlo gave this to Bane Tulku Urgyen Tendzin (*Ba-gNas sPrul-sKu U-rGyan bsTan-'Dzin*). I received the full transmission from both of them.

The nephew of Sherab Membar's nephew was called Urgyen Rangjung (*U-rGyan Rang-Byung*) and his son was Khordong Terchen Nuden Dorje Drophan Lingpa Drolo Tsal (*Nus-lDan rDo-rJe 'Gro-Phan gLing-Pa Gro-Lod rTsal*). He is the Speech incarnation of Nanam Dorje Dudjom (*sNa-Nam rDo-rJe bDud-'Joms*), the incarnation of Khyeu-Chung Lotsawa's Body and the incarnation of Padmasambhava's Mind. The text YANG-GSANG RDO-RJE GRO-LOD KYI GTER-LUNG says, "*Nuden Dorje has the special blessing of Nanam Dorje's Speech and of Khyeu-Chung Lotsawa's Body. You are my [Padmasambhava's] heart son and in future times you will be great due to revealing treasure teachings and objects[1].*"

At Ko-Ko-Nor and other great places he revealed seven Guru Thongwa Donden (*Guru mThong-Ba Don-lDan*) statues which are the sKu-rTen, the representatives, of Padmasambhava's Body; eleven stones which are called Dodrom Thongwa Donden (*rDo-Drom mThong-Ba Don-lDan*), each five spans in diameter and with Padmasambhava's handprint on the top and the finger mark of Yeshe Tsogyal impressed right around the middle. These stones are about three inches high, of rare appearance and, although originally green in colour, they turn maroon, black and so on during meditation. He also revealed twenty-seven other treasure stones.

As Sungten (*gSung-rTen*), the representatives of Padmasambhava's Speech, he revealed the following texts: PHYI-SGRUB BKA'-BRGYAD, BLA-SGRUB, NANG-SGRUB MKHA'-'GRO, GSANG-DRUB ZHI-KHRO LTA-BA KLONG-YANGS, YANG-GSANG GRO-LOD, GSER-CHOS, ZAB GSANG MKHA-'GRO SANG-MDZOD. He also revealed DRAG-PO LHA-NGA and sKu-GSUM ZHI-KHRO.

As the thugten (*Thugs-rTen*), the representative of Padmasambhava's Mind, he revealed the PHURPA NANGSRI ZILNON (*Phur-Pa sNang-Srid Zil-gNon*) along with ten phurpa made of sky iron from the heart of a dragon and a Hung made of sky iron which Padmasambhava held at Samye.

The first reincarnation of Nuden Dorje was born two years after his death. He was known as Chagkung Geuter (*LCags-Khung sGe'u gTer*) or Gili Terton (*Gili gTer-sTon*) or Dudjom Lingpa (*bDud-'Joms gLing-Pa*).

The second incarnation was called Dorje Gya (*rDo-rJe rGya*). He was born in Yu Khog district. He was the son of Terchen Zhenpen Lingpa (*gTer-Chen gZhan-Phan gLing-Pa*). He revealed two volumes of treasure teaching (*gTer-Chos*), one of Khandro (*mKha'-'Gro*) and one of Dzogchen (*rDzogs-Chen*).

The third, sometimes counted as the fourth, incarnation is myself. This very small man who looks like a firefly has been given a name like the sun, namely Khordong Terchen Chime Rigdzin Wangpo (*'Khor-gDong gTer-chen 'Chi-Med Rig-'Dzin dBang-Po*). When I was three I entered on the dharma. When I was five I learned reading and spelling and for the next nine years until I was thirteen I studied with the five great reincarnate lamas of that monastery including Bane Tulku Genlo (*Ba-gNas sPrul-sKu Gan-Lo*), Tulku Gyurme Dorje (*sPrul-sKu 'Gyur-Med rDo-rJe*), Tulku Kunzang Dorje (*sPrul-sKu Kun-bZang rDo-rJe*) and Tulku Pema Namzang (*sPrul-sKu Padma rNam-bZang*). Moreover thirteen or fourteen old monks helped me with study so I had a good chance to learn.

Notes

[1] For an example of his writing see Low, J. BEING RIGHT HERE: THE MIRROR OF CLEAR MEANING, (Shambala Publications, 2004).

12

Education in
Khordong Monastery

In brief, whoever comes to the monastery to enter the religious life is taught the alphabet, reading and writing. The entrants usually come at about the age of five but I have also seen them above the age of eighteen. Also in my monastery there were two or three monks who had never learned to read and write but who had memorised all the necessary texts and had studied and practised well. Their learning was not less than that of other monks and they spent almost all the time in practice since they were not distracted by reading books on history and so on.

The children begin their education with reading and spelling and then they learn some verses of praise to Manjusri called GANG BLO MA. We believe that by reading this the children will develop better memories and more intelligence. Memorising texts is important for many reasons. If a text is in your memory you can recite it under any circumstances, including in total darkness. The texts fill the children with beautiful words, images and rhythms, as well as making them part of a tradition. Students are introduced to each text by having it read to them, so that they experience the transmission of the sound, lung (*rLung*). After that they start memorising the CHOS-sPYOD RAB-GSAL which contains over two hundred pages of prayers and Buddhist instruction. This text is the basic deity practice of all the monks in the monastery. When that is mastered they start to memorise the Jangter practices of *sGro-Ba Kun-Grol* focussed on Chenresi, *Rig-'Dzin gDung-sGrub* focussed on Padmasambhava and *Thugs-sGrub Drag-Po-rTsal* focussed on a wrathful aspect of Padmasambhava. Memorising these frequently used texts is necessary because the monks are not allowed to look at their texts during the main parts of the practices of extensive ritual visualisation.

Traditional Tibetan education and modern education are very different. For example, in the modern system all school education must be finished within about twelve years but in the Tibetan system the students continue to study until they have mastered their studies, whether it takes ten or twenty or even forty years. This was possible because in East Tibet the monks had no need to get a job and if there is no need to get a job, then there is no question of needing to quickly gain a qualification.

The education provided in the monastery was purely for Dharma and not for any other reason and so the only texts used were Dharma texts. Moreover in strict monasteries such as Khordong, Bane (*Ba-gNas*), Dodrubchen (*mDo-Grub-Chen*), Dzogchen, Dorje Drag and so on even the study of poetry, for example the Kavyadarsha by Dandin, was not allowed. This was because many poems were about love which was held to be disturbing for monks. Also history and legends, either of Tibet or of other countries, were not allowed. Even very high Dharma stories were not permitted until all studies were finished because the students might then be tempted away from the necessary Dharma studies by these other texts which were easier to read.

Now as regards the main texts studied for Sutra and general Buddhism, the *Dul-Ba mDo rTsa-Ba* and the *So-So-Thar-Pai mDo* and others were used for the Vinaya, the study of monastic rules. The main texts on logic and analysis were the *Pramanavarttika* and the other six famous texts by Dharmakirti. We also studied the *mNgon-rTogs-rGyan* and the rest of the famous five texts of Maitreyanath. For Madhyamika we studied the *dBu-Ma rTsa-Ba Shes-Rab*, the *dBu-Ma-rGyan* and others. For Abhidharma we studied the *mNgon-Pa mDzod* and the *mNgon-Pa sDus-Pa* and others.

Students had to give detailed attention to the *Bodhicaryavatara* (*Byang-Chub Sems-dPa'i sPyod-Pa La 'Jug-Pa*) and the other root Indian texts found in the thirteen volumes of the traditional Nyingma study programme. For Tantra the texts used are the GSANG-SNGAGS LAM-RIM by Padmasambhava, the CHOS-DBYINGS MDZOD and the rest of the MDZOD BDUN by Longchenpa, the KUN-BZANG BLA-MAI ZHAL-LUNG by Patrul Rinpoche and the SNGAGS-RIM of Pema Trinle. The YE-SHES BLA-MA and DGONGS-PA ZANG-THAL were used for teaching Dzogchen.

There was no entrance fee or course fee for studying; the only things the students needed to provide were the books for their own use. In East Tibet all the monks, even the poorest, had sufficient food and clothing and did not have to use their education to gain these things. However in Central Tibet, some government or semi-government service might be necessary.

The period of teaching ran from the eighth month to the fifth month of the following year. The teaching was done by the Khenpo (*mKhan-Po*) scholars, specialist Khenpos, high Lamas and other experts. Whoever wished to hear the teaching was allowed to attend but if, for example, there were one hundred people present, perhaps only fifty would really study, while the rest were thinking that attending was part of their religious duty and that by doing this every day some Dharma would continue for them. Those who had studied well were called Lopon (*sLob-dPon*), or Kyorpon (*sKyor-dPon*), assistant professor or teacher. At the monastery there were some scholars who had studied the same texts fifty or more times; since there was no age- or year-limit, scholars could attend the same teachings again and again. For that reason there was no question of pass or fail. Those who became experts or were acknowledged by many monasteries to have understood, were considered to have passed.

From cockcrow in the morning until 12 o'clock at night the students pursued their studies. Teaching was given from 5 a.m. until 2 p.m. Perhaps three or four Khenpos would be giving different teachings. This gives you a general account of our system of education.

They were extra subjects such as medicine, architecture for stupas, for mandalas, for monasteries and other buildings, as well as painting, statue-making and so on. The text used for this is the BZO-RIG PA-TRA, ARTS EDUCATION, by Mi-Pham Rin-Po-Che. Now someone might object that it was stated above that the education was only for Dharma and so how can these other subjects be introduced? But our idea is that medicine is also a part of the Dharma. Out of one hundred doctors, fifty will never take any money for diagnosis or treatment. However if someone should offer doctors such things as medicines or ingredients then they will accept these happily and use them to treat other patients. The subjects and crafts taught in the bZO-RIG PA-TRA are actually only for Dharma. Sometimes the topics look easy and sometimes they look very very difficult.

To become a high scholar like a Kyorpon in East Tibet, or a Geshe (dGe-Shes) in Central Tibet, might take fifteen to twenty years. But if one wishes to gain these levels by modern methods of study it would require more than two hundred years. Now I say this because firstly our teachers would teach one subject for two to three hours, or even for four to five hours if they wished to finish one section or subsection of the text. But in modern education the lesson period is forty-five minutes and at the beginning of the lesson each student has to answer his name for the roll call which can take five to ten minutes, leaving only thirty-five minutes for the actual teaching. Then when the teacher starts to teach he must be always looking at his watch to see how much time he has left and that distracts his attention from teaching, so that in the end the students get only about thirty minutes of instruction.

Secondly, in the modern education system the students only study selected items from here and there and do not work systematically through any book from beginning to end whereas in Tibet the whole text has to be fully understood. Also in Tibet the great teachers did not have to wonder about whether their students would turn up or not because they knew that all the students liked study. The teacher is perhaps fifty years old and he believes that all his students, aged from fifteen to fifty, will come due to their own interest and so he does not need to call the names and check if they are present.

I once spoke about this with a colleague at the university in Santiniketan and he said, "Yes, we have a teacher like that here. One day he started teaching at 3 p.m. He was famous and very much respected and his audience paid attention. At 9 p.m. the janitor came and said, 'Sir, my duty is finished and now I have to lock up.' And then the teacher checked his watch and ended the lesson." But there are not many teachers like that and so I say that what was possible in twenty years in Tibet would take two hundred years in the modern system.

I do not say anything here about relative degrees of intelligence but merely that the teaching systems are like that. Also in Tibet the teachers became great scholars because they were paid no salary and so they focussed only on their study for the benefit of their own and others' understanding. However in the modern system even professors need money and so we cannot really know if they are good scholars who love learning for its own sake.

Students did not need to pay fees to the monastery for their education and they were also free of any worries about food and lodging since, from the moment of starting in the monastery, they received everything free of charge. Those who were from big houses would be sponsored all their lives and the families of some monks would even sponsor other monks every year. In this way poor monks would get food and other necessities either directly from the monastery or from some rich people. For example at Khordong Monastery there was a monk called Pema Legden (*Padma Legs-dDan*), who was not a very high monk, but his family was middle-class and he would give food and education to the new scholars for their first four to five years. He liked to live a little outside the monastery because the young monks made a lot of noise of reciting their texts. In Tibet there was a saying, *"Chos-Pa Ri La sDud Na Zan Gong Gyen La Ril"*, *"Even if a Dharma practitioner lives at the top of a mountain, food will roll uphill to him."*

13

Khordong Monastery: Annual Cycle of Rituals

I will describe the rituals of worship and meditation that were performed each year at Khordong Monastery from the time of Sherab Membar (*Shes-Rab Me-'Bar*) until I was twenty years of age. In general the rituals followed the system of Dorje Drag Monastery in Central Tibet, which is the head monastery of the Jangter tradition.

SOME IMPORTANT DAYS CELEBRATED DURING THE YEAR

The 1st month after losar (*Lo-gSar*), the new year, is generally known in Tibet as Dawa Dangpo (*Zla-Ba Dang-Po*), meaning 'first month'. In the Nyingmapa system it is known as the Rabbit Month. According to the Hor or Mongolian system it is the Ta (*rTa*) or Horse Month. In the village system prevalent all over Tibet it is referred to as the Birth Month. However whatever its name, there is no doubt that it is the 1st month of the year. It is also called 'Chotrul Dawa' (*Chos-'Phrul Zla-Ba*), month of miracles.

On the 15th day of this month Lord Buddha Shakyamuni showed his compassionate magic power in order to control and help the six Tirthikas, non-Buddhist adepts.

Early in the morning on the 7th day of the 6th month, or Saga Dawa (*Sa-Ga Zla-Ba*), the Buddha was born. On the 15th day of 6th month he both gained enlightenment in the morning and, many years later, died in the night. In the 3rd month on the 15th day the SRI KALACHAKRA TANTRA was first taught. On the 4th day of the 6th Tibetan month Lord Buddha came into Mayadevi's womb and this is also the day of the dharmacakra pravartana, the 'first turning of the wheel of the dharma', the first teaching of the doctrine by Buddha Shakyamuni. The 22nd day of the 9th month is celebrated as the great time of the descent of the divine, lhabab duchen (*Lha-Babs Dus-Chen*), the day on which Buddha Shakyamuni descended back to earth from the Tushita Heaven where he had gone to teach the Dharma to his mother. All Tibetans would agree on the details of these stories.

THE FIRST MONTH

On the 1st day of the 1st month there are the celebrations for Losar, New Year, and on the 2nd and 3rd days there are also some New Year celebrations. The 4th to 7th days follow the usual monastery practice. That is, in the morning reciting the CHOCHO RABSAL (CHOS-sPYOD RAB-GSAL), a collection of prayers for daily reading, and reciting the KANGSO (BSKANG-GSO) texts for the reparation of commitments in the afternoon. From the 7th to the 15th there is BDE-CHEN ZHING-sGRUB, the practice and teachings on how to take rebirth in the Buddha Realm of Amitabha. On the 13th the 'KHOR-'DAS sPYI-BSANGS is read to purify all the possible modes of existence. On the 15th there is the initiation of Amitabha with the One Thousand Buddhas. On the morning of the 15th the SOJONG (GSO-sBYONGS) practice of confession and reparation of monastic vows is read in the main temple and in the evening the NGAGSO (sNGAGS-GSO) to repair tantric vows is read.

In other houses in the monastery some monks practise the sGYU-'PHRUL BKA'-MA, the oral tradition of the illusory nature according to the text by Pema Trinle (*Padma 'Phrin-Las*). Then the general body of the monks follow the usual monastic practice from the 19th to the 25th days.

On the 25th the one hundred monks in the new Lhabrang Serkhang (*Lha-Brang gSer-Khang*) perform the KHANDRO SANGWA YESHE (MKHA-'GRO GSANG-BA YE-SHES), Secret Wisdom Dakini ritual, according to the system of Dorje Drag and they perform the associated *Jinseg* (*Byin-bSregs*) fire ritual. If some great lama is sick then they will also perform the *mKha-'Gro Gar-'Cham* dakini ritual dance with the *mKha-'Gro bSu-bZlog*, the ritual for dispelling difficulties, and the *brTen-Zhugs*, prayers for long life.

From the 26th to the 28th there is the usual monastic practice. On the 29th the *Khandro Sangwa Yeshe* is practised along with its associated *Sudog* (*bSu-bZlog*) ritual for repelling difficulties. If that is not done, then we do the *Phurba*, Tantric Nail ritual of Gonpo Wangyal (*mGon-Po dBang-rGyal*) with its dogpa ritual for repelling difficulties. On the 30th the *Sojong* is read in the morning and the *Ngagso* in the evening.

THE SECOND MONTH

The second month is generally known as the Dog Month. In the Hor system it is known as the Snake Month and the Nyingmapa call it the Dragon Month. On its 10th day, Tsechu (*Tshes-bCu*), there is *Phyi-sGrub bLa-Ma bKa'-brGyad*, the outer ritual practice of the eight great deities. Preparation for this starts on the 8th and 9th. This is a Tersar (*gTer-gSar*), new treasure text, of my first incarnation, Khordong Terchen Nuden Dorje Drophan Lingpa Drolo Tsal (*'Khor-gDong gTer-Chen Nus-lDan rDo-rJe 'Gro-Phan gLing-Pa Gro-Lod rTsal*).

On the morning of the 15th there is *Sojong* and the *Gyuntsog* (*rGyun-Tshogs*) ritual of many different offerings. This follows the Dorje Drag (*rDo-rJe Brag*) system coming from the translator Vairocana, Kunrig Nampar Nangdze (*Kun-Rigs rNam-Par sNang-mDzad*). On the afternoon of the 15th the *Ngagso* from the text *Rigdzin Tsasum Kundu* (*Rig-'Dzin rTsa-gSum Kun-'Dus*) the assembly of the vidyadharas and the three roots, is read. On the 25th the *Cham* (*'Cham*) or ritual dance practice starts at the monastery of Serlog Gang (*gSer-Log sGang*) which is about two kilometres from the main monastery. There the dancing master, the cymbal master and some experienced monks teach dancing to the novices. Also on the 25th day the *Tersar Khandro Sangwa Yeshe* is read and in the Serkang (*gSer-Khang, golden house*) room the ritual of the deity Demchog (*bDe-mChog, great bliss*) is performed.

On the 29th day Gonpo Wangyal's ZABTIG PHURBA (ZAB-THIG PHUR-PA), profound ritual nail practice, is read. On the morning of the no-moon day the SOJONG and the GYUNTSOG are read and in the afternoon the NGAGSO is read.

The first month is more active than the second in terms of large ceremonies of ritual worship. In the second month whenever they are not reading any special texts, all the monks are required to assemble in the main hall to read the full CHOCHO RABSAL daily practice text in the morning and the KANGSO (BsKANG-GSO) for reparation of commitments in the afternoon.

THE THIRD MONTH

The third month is generally called the Pig Month, while the Hor system calls it the Horse Month and the Nyingmapa refer to it as the Snake Month.

On the 10th day, with the Vajracharya directing, one hundred monks make one hundred TSOG (TSHOGS) offerings according to the ZHITRO TAWA LONGYANG (ZHI-KHRO LTA-BA KLONG-YANGS), the Terchö of Khordong Terchen Nuden Dorje. This practice includes the forty-two peaceful and fifty-eight wrathful forms and also the ten vidyadharas with consorts, Rigdzin Yabyum (Rig-'Dzin Yab-Yum), and the whole Phurba Dorje Zhonu (Phur-Pa rDo-rJe gZhon-Nu). It is performed in the house of Nuden Dorje. Then on the next day these one hundred monks go to Serlog Gang, and putting up tents, they stay there till the 15th. Here they read the ZHITRO four times a day and they also do one thousand NEDREN (gNAS-'DREN) to lead the dead to a good rebirth. This is especially for all the villagers in that area who have died in the last year as well as for all the animals that have died and for all the insects and other creatures that have been killed by the villagers in the course of their work. The Zhitro Nyerpa steward (Zhi-Khro gNyer-Pa) of this practice arranges the finances for these rituals and many people send offerings from up to one thousand miles away.

On the 8th day of the 3rd month, in the Lhabrang temple of the New Serkhang, the practice for Sri Kalachakra commences with the SACHOG (SA-CHOG) ritual to prepare the site. Then on the 9th day there is the TAGON (LTA-GON), initial stage of the initiation, and then the KHYILKHOR DULTSON (DKHYIL-'KHOR RDUL-TSHON) mandala made with coloured powder is created. On the 14th and 15th days, one hundred and twenty-five monks practise Sri Kalachakra and on the 15th day they perform the *Jinseg* fire ritual and the *Dagjug* (*bDag-'Jug*) ritual of self-empowerment as the deity. Inside the Serkhang they perform the *Dorje Gar* (*rDo-rJe Gar*) ritual dance which may only be witnessed by those who have received the Sri Kalachakra initiation. By alternation, one year Mipham (*Mi-Pham*) Rinpoche's *Kalachakra* text will be read and then the next year the *Terchö* (*gTer-Chos*) of Lerab Lingpa (*Las-Rab gLing-Pa*) will be used.

On the 15th day some monks read the *Sojong*. Also on that day one hundred and fifty monks read the *Tsokle Rinchen Trengwa* (*Tshogs-Las Rin-Chen 'Phreng-Ba*) ritual of offering the body. Then, with other monks, they make the *Torma Gyatsa* (*gTor-Ma brGya-rTsa*) offering of one hundred ritual sacrifices with the water offering. Also on that day four or six of these monks must go to the Ro-Nye River, which is about two miles from the monastery. There they read mainly the *Prajnaparamita* texts. Originally only these texts were taken but later on several volumes of the *Kangyur* (*bKa'-'Gyur*) collected works of the Buddha were also taken. There they ritually offer blessed water into the whirlpools in the river. When they return they perform *Gawa Khyilpa* (*dGa'-Ba 'Khyil-Pa*) whirling happiness dancing in the monastery courtyard.

Then from the 25th until new moon day, with the Dorje Lopon Tripa (*rDo-rJe sLob-dPon Khri-Pa*) head of meditative rituals himself directing, one hundred monks in the New Serkhang recite the ritual of the peaceful and wrathful deities, the *Zhitro Tsorwa Rangdrol* (*Zhi-Khro Tshor-Ba Rang-Grol*) of Karma Lingpa along with one hundred nedren for the dead. This is sponsored by the people from Nye village.

On new moon day in the morning the monks read the *Sojong* to repair their vinaya vows and the *Ngagso* in the afternoon. There are also some extra activities in this month. On the 20th there is a dance rehearsal and examination held in the grounds of Serlog Gang. Either the Umdze (*dBu-mDzad*) choirmaster is there or else his assistant, together with the dancing-master or his assistant, and one of the two Geko (*dGe-bsKos*) disciplinarians. Then each new dancer stands between two experienced dancers and together they practise all the steps and gestures. If all the novices pass on that first day then they will be allowed to appear in the NGACHAM (*rNGA-'CHAM*) drum dance on the next *Tsechu* (*Tshes-bCu*), tenth day of the lunar calendar. They would already have had about twenty-five days' practice and also have done preliminary practice in the Sartra (*Sar Tra*) beginners' section.

On the 20th another important activity occurs when some very careful monks take out from boxes the stored sections of the huge embroidered thangka-hanging and reassemble it. The whole thangka is about 50 metres high and 20 metres wide. On the 25th day the Vajracharya with twenty-five monks perform the *TSECHU SACHOG* (*TSHES-BCU SA-CHOG*), preparing the ground for the 10th day celebrations the following month. From the 26th to the 29th Tormas are made by fifty monks and also some experts construct the mandala with coloured powders. On the new moon day the final rehearsal for the lama dancing is held in the temple courtyard. This is also an examination and some who passed the earlier test will fail here. This concludes the activities of the third month.

THE FOURTH MONTH

The fourth month is generally known as the Rat Month (*Byi-Ba*). In the Hor system it is known as the Sheep Month, and the Nyingmapa call it the Horse Month.

On the first day the Torma for the practice of *LAMA SANGDU* (*bLA-MA gSANG-'DUs*), the secret assembly of Guru Padmasambhava, are made in the Upper Serkhang. Then on the third day in the New Serkhang, the Dorje Lopon Chenpo and one hundred and twenty-five monks read the *GYALNGEN LASANG* (*rGYAL-bRNGAN LHA-bSANG*) while smoke offerings are made. After they have finished this they make the hanging frames and fit the ropes for the huge thangka that had been assembled in the third month. While the frame is being assembled the one hundred and eight volumes of the *KANGYUR* are opened and each volume is gone through using the Dzog (*rDzog*) system of turning each page. Then the monks go to the four directions and read the *HEART SUTRA* (*PRAJNAPARAMITA HRIDAYA*) with the *DOGPA* repelling ritual. This reading must be continued until the frame is finished. They then carry the *KANGYUR* around the monastery and then put each of the volumes back in its own place.

This recitation and *Dogpa* is done because formerly at Nyi-Dar monastery about fifty miles to the west of Khordong Monastery there had been a monk who became a demon when he died and who then always tried to cause trouble for Nyingma practitioners. One year he broke the supporting beam of the frame and this resulted in the death of one man. Replacement beams are difficult to obtain quickly. When the thangka is hung in the new monastery hall it is given *RABNE* (*RAB-GNAS*) consecration because, although it has received this before, it has just been taken out of the box where it had been packed at the end of the ritual the previous year. The thangka could be fully displayed since the hall was very large but some of the border cloth at the top and at the bottom had to be rolled up.

From the 3rd day the *RIGDZIN DUNGDRUB DRUBCHEN* (*RIG-'DZIN GDUNG-SGRUB SGRUB-CHEN*), the Jangter inner practice of Padmasambhava, commenced. In some years the making of *TENDU RILBU* (*brTan-Du Ril-Bu*) pills for stability is combined with this practice and if this is done then at the finish of the practice, on the 9th day the *RANGJUNG KAWANG CHENMO* (*RANG-'BYUNG BKA'I-DBANG CHEN-MO*), the great initiation of self-existing speech, is given. However if the rilbu pills are not made then on the 10th day, tsechu, there is the cham dance of the *DUNGDRUB TSENGYE* (*GDUNG-SGRUB MTSHAN-BRGYAD*), the practice of the eight forms of Padmasambhava.

While some of the monks are reading the *RIGDZIN DUNGDRUB* in the New Serkhang, one hundred and twenty-five monks are with the Dorje Lopon reading the *LAMA SANGDU* of Guru Chöwang (*Gu-Ru Chos-dBang*). If not making Rilbu Pills, then when the *CHAM* dance is finished, the *DUMBU ZHI WANG* (*DUM-BU-BZHI DBANG*), initiation in four parts by four implements, is given in the afternoon.

For this ten or eleven day period the sponsorship used to be offered by the house of Terchen Nuden Dorje and until I was fifteen years old the activities during these days were sponsored by my own house because we received many offerings and remunerations for pujas and other activities. Our sponsorship was to purify the receiving of offerings for performing dharma activities. The funds were administered by the Tsechu Nyerpa (*Tshes-bCu gNyer-Pa*) steward.

On the 8th day one thousand *TSOG* offerings were made and also one thousand butterlamps. This day was financed by Sherab Chödro

(*Shes-Rab Chos-Grogs*). On the 10th day one thousand *Tsog* offerings were made and one thousand butterlamps and this was sponsored by the house of the second Nuden Dorje. For these two days the minimum was one thousand *Tsog* offerings and one thousand butter-lamps but around six to seven thousand *Tsog* were possible since everybody wished to make offerings on these days. When the *Rildrup* (*Ril-sGrub*) sacred pill-making is performed then some extra days preparation [for *Sa-Chog, Ta-Gon* etc] connected with that are sponsored by Nuden Dorje's house. On the 8th day at sunset the *Tsasum Torma* (*rTsa-gSum gTor-Ma*) sacrificial cakes for the Three Roots are made and then offered with *Kuntag Gyalmo* (*Kun-brTag rGyal-Mo*) dancing.

The first day's system is that of Dorje Drag and the ninth day's system is that seen by Nuden Dorje with his own eyes when he went to Zang-dopalri. About five hundred yards of cloth were put up as a huge awning for the monastery courtyard because each year there is the possibility of some rain falling on the monastery. The rain only falls on an area of about five miles around the monastery. The awning was necessary because Gonpo Wangyal would not allow rain-stopping rituals to be practised during these days. This was because, in order to prepare the ground for the arrival of the Tsengye (*mTsan-brGyad*) eight manifestations of Padmasambhava, Indra, Brahma and the nagas send rain to purify the area.

On the 9th day there is a final rehearsal during which the lamas dance wearing their usual monk's dress. This *Sorig Cham* (*gSo-Rigs 'Cham*) healing dance, or *Mar Cham* (*dMar 'Cham*) red robes dance was formerly the rehearsal and test but nowadays the rehearsals have already been concluded in the third month. Yet although it is not really necessary it is continued for the sake of custom. On this day only the dancers and the musicians are allowed to be present.

On the afternoon of the 9th day inside the large awning, many canopies large and small, with cloth hangings, pendants, banners and so on are hung up as decorations. On the 10th day all the monks arise in the morning before cock-crow at the first *Nyensan* (*sNyan-bSan*) tune of invitation played on the Gyaling oboe. At the second Nyensan, they come to the verandah of the main temple. At the third Nyensan they start reading the *Rigdzin Dungdrub* and by about 5 o'clock the first section is finished and then they take tea and breakfast. Then they read the LE'U DUNMA (LE'U-BDUN-MA) prayer in seven chapters by Padmasambhava followed by the TOPA (BSTOD-PA) praise to the Dharma Protectors. They read the KANGWA (BSKANG-BA) repairing of broken vows, reading the text up to the section called TSASIIM KANGSO (RTSA-GSUM BSKANG-GSO) repairing commitments to the Three Roots, by which time the sun is almost rising, and then the dancing commences.

On the 11th day the monks all assemble early at about 5 a.m. They read the whole text of the RIGDZIN DUNGDRUB and then they each receive the RILDRUP RABJAM (Ril-sGrub Rab-'Byams-Ka'i dBang), pervasive speech initiation, or if not that, then the DUMPOZHI initiation (ZLUM-PO-BZHI DBANG) which is given with vase, skull, mirror and Torma. If the RILBU practice has been performed then at this point there is a fire ritual and then some of the ash from the fire and the mandala coloured-powder is taken down to the river, and at a given sign from the monastery, is put into the whirlpools while at the monastery the GAKHYI dance is performed three times and the snake gods are requested to remain peaceful.

From the 11th to the 15th day one hundred and eight monks in the New Serkhang read the TSE-SGRUB BDUD-RTSI 'KHYIL-PA BUM-SGRUB, a long-life practice of the deity Dutsi Kyilwa. The New Lhabrang sponsors this for two days, the Dratshang (Gvra Tshang) general monastery school sponsors it for one day, the village people for one day, and the nomads for one day.

On the morning of the 12th day most monks do their usual practice but some make the RABNE TORMA (RAB-GNAS GTOR-MA) for the consecration and prepare the mandalas and put the thangka in the central hall.

From the 13th to the 15th day one hundred and eight monks together with the Dorje Lopon read the ritual text RABNE GYUDON GYAMTSHO (RAB-GNAS RGYUD-DON RGYA-MTSHO) which consecrates the items indicated. For all the statues and other sacred items in the monastery and for the village gods and mountain gods they make TRÜSOL ('KHRUS-GSOL) purification and RABNE consecration blessing. During that time the ordinary monks read the KANJUR, the collected teachings of the Buddha. If some high monk had died then his family might sponsor lamps and also the reading of the KANGYUR.

On the 15th there is the *Sojong* in the morning and the *Ngagso* in the afternoon.

From the 16th to the 24th day the monks follow the general monastery practice system.

On the 25th the Torma for the New Treasure, *Khacho Dorje Naljorma* (*gTer-gSar mKha'-sPyod rDo-rJe rNal-'Byor-Ma*) are prepared and then that ritual of the goddess Vajrayogini is performed.

From the 26th to the 28th day the general monastery system is followed.

On the 28th the ritual cakes are made for the *Magyud Traglungma* (*Ma-rGyud Khrag-rLung-Ma*) vital essence of the mother tantras. On the 29th day that puja is performed and the Torma are thrown away.

On the 30th there is *Sojong* in the morning and *Ngagso* in the evening.

The Fifth Month

The fifth month is generally known as the Ox Month. In the Hor system it is known as the Monkey Month, and the Nyingmapa call it the Sheep Month. In this month there is an important Tsechu tenth day celebration of Padmasambhava at Tsone (*Tso-gNas*).

At the monastery on the 8th day in the New Serkhang sixteen monks read the *Kunrig Nampar Nangdze* Vairocana practice.

On the 10th day in the monastery hall there is the Tsechu practice of Tamdrin Dregpa Zilnon (*rTa-mGrin Dregs-Pa Zil-gNon*), a wrathful form which controls demons. This is a terma of Nuden Dorje.

On the morning of the 15th there is the *Sojong* and then all the monks go out from the monastery to three nearby places: Lagyal Gyugmo (*kLa-rGyal Gyug-Mo*), Mochog (*rMog-Chog*) and Lake Gyagangtso (*rGya-sGang mTso*). There they recite the *Dzamling Chisang* ('*Dzam-gLing sPyi-bSang*) smoke offering to purify the world, and also the *Khorde Chisang* ('*Khor-'Das sPyi-bSang*) smoke offering to purify samsara and nirvana, a terma of Gonpo Wangyal.

Then from the 16th to the 18th day they stay near the lake and relax and on the 19th day they again come near the lake and do the *Khorde Chisang*.

On the 25th day they are back at the monastery and recite the ritual of the wrathful lion-headed dakini SENGEDONG DRAGMO (SENG-GE GDONG DRAG-MO), the terma of Mati Ratna, and they make many collected TSOG offerings with it

On the 29th day they read the TARDOG (GTAR-BZLOG), the repelling obstacles section of that SENGE DONGMA text.

On the new moon day there is SOJONG in the morning and NGAGSO in the afternoon.

THE SIXTH MONTH

The sixth month is generally known as the Tiger Month. In the Hor system it is known as the Bird Month, and the Nyingmapa call it the Monkey Month.

As stated above on the 4th day of this month the Buddha came into the womb of Mayadevi and on that day the monks read the NECHU CHAGCHOD (GNAS-BCU PHYAG-MCHOD) praise of the sixteen Arhants according to the Jangter system, and they read the KANGYUR.

On the 8th day there is the practice of the MENLAI DOCHOG YIZHIN WANGYAL (SMAN-BLA'I MDO-CHOG YID-BZHIN DBANG-RGYAL), the powerful wish-fulfilling practice of the eight Medicine Buddhas written by the 5th Dalai Lama.

On the 10th day there is the Dorje Drolo practice TERSAR DROLO (GTER-GSAR GRO-LOD) which is a treasure text of Nuden Dorje. On the 15th there is SOJONG in the morning and NGAGSO in the evening. Then the Yarne (DBYAR-GNAS) summer rainy-season retreat begins.

On the 17th day there is the Zilnon Sengdongma Suchog (Zil-gNon Seng-gDong-Ma bSu-Chog) welcoming ritual for the Lion-headed Dakini. On the 19th day the sixty Torma offerings DRUCHUMA (DRUG-CU-MA) from this SENGE DONGMA cycle are performed.

On the 23rd day there is the ZILNON SENGDONG PHURDRUB (ZIL-GNON SENG-GDONG PHUR-SGRUB) ritual nail practice associated with this Lion-headed Dakini cycle. It has sections on CHAMKAR (LCAGS-MKHAR) imprisoning iron enclosure, Do (MDOS) protective thread constructions, and TSANGDRUB (RTSANG-SGRUB) snaring.

On the 25th there is a ritual of TSOG assembled offerings for the Dakini Sengdongma. On the 29th the thread constructions, the iron enclosure, the snares and the ritual Torma cakes are all thrown away.

On the new moon there is *Sojong* in the morning and *Ngagso* in the afternoon. The other days of the month follow the general monastery ritual system.

THE SEVENTH MONTH

This month is generally known as the Rabbit Month. In the Hor system it is known as the Dog Month and the Nyingmapa call it the Bird Month.

On the 8th day the monks on the Yarne summer rainy-season retreat read the *TASHI SOJONG* (*bKRA-SHIS bSO-sBYONG*) auspicious confession and reparation. On the 10th day the *DRA DRAGMAR TER* (*GVRA DRAG-MAR gTER*) Treasure of the Fierce Red Corner found by Gonpo Wangyal is read with assembled *Tsog* offerings. On the 15th there is *Sojong* in the morning and *Ngagso* in the afternoon. On the 25th day assembled *Tsog* offerings are made on the basis of the *MAGYUD TRAGLUNG*. On the 29th day the *SANGPHUR* (*gSANG-PHUR*) Secret Nail Terma of Gonpo Wangyal is read.

On the 30th day *Sojong* is read in the morning and *Ngagso* in the afternoon. This day marks the end of the summer rainy-season retreat and for the next three days the monks relax and stay freely outside the monastery.

THE EIGHTH MONTH

This eighth month is generally known as the Dragon Month. In the Hor system it is known as the Pig Month and the Nyingma call it the Dog Month.

On the 7th day dancing practice commences. On the 8th day the *DONYO CHIPA* (*DON-YOD mCHIS-PA*) Meaningful Dwelling of Nuden Dorje is read. The Tsechu Tsog ritual offered on the 10th day is taken from the text of the *KABGYE DRAGPO RANGJUNG RANGSHAR* (*bKA'-brGYAD DRAG-PO RANG-BYUNG RANG-SHAR*), the Self-existing Self-arising Eight Wrathful Forms, a treasure Ter of Rigdzin Godem. From the 10th until the 15th one thousand *KANGWA* (*bsKANG-BA*) are read in the Lhabrang Serkhang to repair and replenish our relationship with the Dharma Protectors.

On the 15th day *Sojong* is read in the morning and *Ngagso* in the afternoon. The final dancing rehearsal is held on the 17th. From the 21st to the 25th one hundred thousand Tsog assembled offerings are made in the Lhabrang using the Jangter Phurba. Then from the 26th to the 29th there is more practice on Phurba with one thousand KANGSO reparations of vows. On the 29th there is the ritual dance of the PHURBA CHAM.

On the 30th SOJONG is read in the morning and NGAGSO in the afternoon.

THE NINTH MONTH

The ninth month is generally known as the Snake Month. In the Hor system it is known as the Rat Month and the Nyingmapa call it the Pig Month.

On the 8th day there is the Menla (sMan-bLa) Medicine Buddha practice. Tsechu puja on the 10th is the SANGPHUR VAJRAKILAYA practice of Gonpo Wangyal.

On the 15th day SOJONG is read in the morning and NGAGSO in the afternoon. We believe that on that day when Lord Buddha was in Tushita he promised to come down to benefit all beings in this world system. If any important lama has died that year or the previous year, then on that day many prayers are said requesting them to come back into the world for the benefit of beings.

On the 22nd day the Buddha came down from Tushita and on that day we read the NETEN CHAGCHOD (gNas-brTan Phyag-mChod) honouring the sixteen Arhants, using the Dorje Drag system.

On the 25th day the ZILNON SENGE DONGMA is read with one hundred Tsog offerings. On the 29th day Gonpo Wangyal's SANGPHUR is read. With that practice the Gyedre Karwa (rGyad-'Dre Kar-Ba) grains are thrown to enchant the eight groups of potentially disturbing spirits.

On the 30th day SOJONG is read in the morning and NGAGSO in the afternoon.

THE TENTH MONTH

The tenth month is generally known as the Horse Month. In the Hor system it is known as the Ox Month and the Nyingmapa call it the Rat Month.

On the 8th day there is *Kunrig* (*Kun-Rig*) Vairocana practice according to the Jangter tradition. On the 10th day a ritual dance practice starts. The Tsechu practice on the 10th day is the *Rigdzin Dungdrub Guru Yonten Terdzod* (*Rig-'Dzin gDung-sGrub Gu-Ru Yon-Tan gTer-mDzod*), a practice focussing on Padmasambhava and which is a treasure text of Rigdzin Godem.

From the 11th to the 15th the *Zhitro Tawa Longyang* (*Zhi-Khro dTa-Ba kLong-Yangs*) text on the peaceful and wrathful deities discovered as a treasure by Nuden Dorje is practised with *Netong* (*gNas-sTong*), emptying the realms of samsara. On the 15th *Sojong* is read in the morning and *Ngagso* in the afternoon.

On the 7th day there is the *Sachog* ritual for preparing the site for whichever practice is to be done in the 10th month of that year. In the six female years the practice is the *Kabgye Rangjung Rangshar* (*bKa'-brGyad Rang-Byung Rang-Shar*) of Rigdzin Godem and in the six male years the texts in the *Shinje Tsedag* (*gShin-rJe Tshe-bDag*) from Gya Zhangtrom (*rGya-Zhang Khrom*) is read. Also on the 7th day there is the first rehearsal of the *Cham* ritual dance. The final rehearsal is held on the 21st day.

From the 23rd to the 29th the practice for that month as described above is read and on the 29th the Torma are thrown away and the *Cham* ritual dance is performed. This can also be performed in the 12th month. The final day of the *Cham* is held in the monastery hall and is not public. When the Torma are thrown the Dorje Lopon is dressed in the Black Hat costume and he dances the *Zorcham* (*Zor-'Chams*) missile weapon dance.

On the new moon day *Sojong* is read in the morning and *Ngagso* in the afternoon. From this day the period of study and practice begins with the *Danying* (*brDa-rNying*), the study of the traditional form of writing Nyingma texts. For all monks and laymen in general, there is teaching on *Lamai Naljor* (*bLa-Mai rNal-'Byor*) guruyoga and on the *Zernga* (*gZer-lNga*) Five Nails preparatory practice. For monks who have finished their *Ngondro* (*sNgon-'Gro*) preparatory practices there is teaching on *Tsalung* (*rTsa-rLung*) energy yoga, and *Dzogchen* (*rDzog-Chen*). No alteration in the order of study is allowed.

The Eleventh Month

The eleventh month is generally known as the Sheep Month. In the Hor system it is known as the Tiger Month and the Nyingmapa call it the Ox Month.

On the 3rd day there is the ritual of *Thugje Chenpo Sachog* (*rThugs-rje Chen-Po Sa-Chog*) to prepare the site for the rituals of Chenresi. Then there is the setting up of the powder-dust Chenresi mandala. On the 8th day the *Mani Bumdrub* (*Mani 'Bum-sGrub*) recitation of 100,000 mantras of Chenresi is started. On the 10th day one hundred *Tsog* are offered with that practice and when it is finished on the 15th day the *Dagjug* self-empowerment and *Nedren* ritual to ensure a good rebirth are done. Also on the 15th there is the general practice of *Sojong* in the morning and *Ngagso* in the afternoon.

On the 25th day in the Lhabrang Serkhang, there is a practice following the Tsalpa (*Tshal-Pa*) system for the dakini Kachöma (*mKha'-sPyod-Ma*).

On the 29th day there is the Gonpo Wangyal's Guru Dragpo with the throwing of the *Gyedo* (*brGyad-mDos*) thread cross of the eight classes of gods and demons.

On the 30th *Sojong* is read in the morning and *Ngagso* in the evening.

The Twelfth Month

The twelfth month is generally known by the name of Monkey. In the Hor system it is known as the Rabbit Month and the Nyingmapa call it the Tiger Month.

On the 7th day there is a ritual dance practice. On the 8th day the *Aṣṭasāhasrikā Prajñāpāramitā Sūtra, The Perfection of Wisdom in 8,000 Lines*, is read. On the 10th day there is a *Tsog* offering with the ritual practice of *Jampal Naga Raksha* (*'Jams-dPal Na-Ga Raksha*) Manjusri in wrathful form as master of demons, and also a *Laetha Tetrug* (*Las-mTha' gTad-sPrugs*) concluding entrustment and exorcism ritual.

On the 15th *Sojong* is read in the morning and *Ngagso* in the afternoon. Also on this day those who are doing *Ngondro* practice are tested on their capacity in *Phowa* (*'Pho-Ba*) consciousness transference, and are given a TSEWANG (TSHE-DBANG) long-life initiation. Those who are doing Tsalung energy yoga practice are given the TUMMO MEWANG (GTUM-MO ME-DBANG) initiation so that heat and power can be developed. Those who are practising dzogchen receive the NGOTRO (NGO-SPROD) introduction to their own nature.

On the 16th there is SACHOG site blessing and the construction of the powder-dust mandala for whichever of the alternative practices was not done in the 10th month. On the 7th day there is the rehearsal for the CHAM ritual dance. The final rehearsal is on the 21st. The main practice is on the 23rd day. On the 25th day the main practice is done with many gathered offerings and, in the New Lhabrang, the NANGDRUB KHANDRO GONGDÜ (NANG-SGRUB MKHA'-'GRO DGONGS-'DUS), the inner practice of the assembled dakinis is read with TSOG and fire offerings.

On the 28th there is the final rehearsal for the dance. The final dance is on the 29th and then the final Torma are thrown out.

On new moon there is SOJONG in the morning, in the afternoon there is CHIDAG DOGPA ('CHI-BDAG BZLOG-PA) ritual to repel death, and NGAGSO in the evening. At night there is a TSEWANG long life initiation, and at midnight those monks who have been doing rituals for the Dharma-palas do their practice.

Thus one full year's cycle of practice is complete.

14

New Year Celebrations

Losar, or new year, occurs on the *FIRST* day of the Tibetan first month which is called *Chos-'Phrul Zla-Wa*, the month of miracles. In our Khordong monastery, the new year was believed to start with the ending of the last new moon day of the last month of the old year. The young people and the ordinary lay people were happy at this time but for dharma people it was a time to consider impermanence and death and to reflect on how little dharma they had managed to do in the past year and how they would have to struggle much harder in the next.

At *Tho-Rangs sTag-Gi Dus*, that is at the time of the tiger at about 2 a.m. when the black of the sky lightens a little, we start *sNyan-gSang 'Bud-Pa*. That is, we give a sign to the Three Roots [Guru, Deva and Dakini] and to the Three Ratnas [Buddha, Dharma and Sangha] to listen to us, by blowing the *Dung-Chen* long horns and also by blowing the *rGya-gLing* oboe and other instruments. These we played together according to our monastery rule and then the *rGya-gLing* played the tune called *Dru-'Dzin Pho-Brang* three times and this lasts for about one and a half hours.

During the first period, the eight monks known as the *mGon-Khang bsKang-gSo-Ba*, who during the last year have been reading the rituals for the dharma protectors, now perform the *dNgos-Grub Len-Pa* receiving of attainments from the *sGRUB-PA CHEN-PO BKA'-BRGYAD*

DRAG-PO RANG-BYUNG RANG-SHAR. The tulkus (sPrul-sKu, incarnation lamas) of the monastery also perform this.

In the second early morning period the mChod-gYog assistant offering monk brings forward the necessary offerings. One boy with all sense organs perfect and very good health, who has good manners and is from a good family, holds a bowl of Phye-Mar sweetened tsampa and one girl with similar qualities holds a pot of chang home brewed beer. Generally women are not allowed within the monastery but this day is special.

Both the boy and the girl must be between 12-14 years of age. Then Mi Tsering (Mi Tshe-Ring) the Long-living Man comes in looking very old and peaceful accompanied by one man dressed like an Indian sadhu, a wandering holy man. They go before the high lamas and say, "Lha rGyal-Lo!", "Victory to the gods." The 'Dra-dKar sadhu figure says many good words but as a kind of joke such as, "Oh yes, I have come from Vajrasattva." Then all go out apart from the head lama and high tulkus. The Mi Tsering says "bKra-Shis bDe-Legs", good wishes, to them and the boy offers the special tsampa and the girl offers the beer.

The head lama says, "Phun-Sum-Tshogs", "May you get plenty of every-thing" and then says, "Kun-Kyang Bag-Dro sKu-Khams-bZang", "You all must be healthy and at ease." Then the joker sadhu says, "Khyad-Cag brTan-Du bDe-Bar Thob-Par-Shog", "You all must be happy." Then the gSol-dPon, the 'head waiter', offers food to the great incarnations and mKhan-Po and public relations officers. The other monks and gurus are given red potatoes with butter and the 'Dra-dKar says,"You all must be happy!".

In the third part of the early morning, at about 5 a.m., a gong is beaten and all the monks come to the monastery and wait to enter the hall to the sound of conch and drum. The ordinary monks enter first but stay standing. At the verandah of the main hall the vajracharya and the other lamas make prostrations and then they slowly enter the hall and stand at their own places. Then when the music sNyan-gSang 'Bud-Pa is being played, the mahavajracharya, who was myself, is received with incense and bows. When he sits down, everyone else takes their seat. Then they all very slowly read the GSOL DEBS LE'U BDUN MA and drink the daily tea. The lamas of the old house, that is the section coming from Sherab Membar (Shes-Rab Me-'Bar), and the lamas of the new house, that is the section coming from Khordong Terchen ('*Khor-gDong gTer-Chen*), alternate each year in offering khapse (*Khab-Se*) biscuits at this point. Then outside they give scarves (*Kha-bTags*) to the vajracharya and then the lamas and tulkus offer each other scarves and say "*bKra-Shis bDe-Legs*", "*Good wishes*", and present themselves before the vajracharya.

The sun rises at about 8 a.m. and then the vajracharya, the *Pyan-Drangs* recitation and music masters and the *Chos-'Dul* vinaya experts not less than one hundred, go to Terchen's house, to its open courtyard since this practice is not allowed under the roof of the *Lha-Brang*. There they read the Lha-bSang rGyal-sMan which must be finished by 1 p.m..

Near that *Lha-Brang* house and at the spot where Gonpo Wangyal (*mGon-Po dBang-rGyal*) built a temple, and at each surrounding mountain there commences the offering of purifying incense, *Lha-bSangs*. At the courtyard in front of the mountain is a level area and there about two hundred people come carrying juniper branches which they place in a great fire. Offerings of smoke and libation (*gSer-sKyems*) are made to the local gods including Gonpo Chag Drugpa (*mGon-Po Phyag Drug-Pa*), Ekajati (*Lha-Mo Ekajati*), Nyenchen Thanglha (*gNyan-Chen Thang-Lha*).

Eight very good yaks and eight fine horses with white hair at the back of their hooves, eight four-horned goats, eight four-horned sheep, eight black dogs with white on their chests – all of these were actually present as well as pictures of many more. Then when they say, "*Lha rGyal-Lo*", "*Victory to the Gods*", all the village men throw tsampa in the air and all the women pour chang. They do this three times and this is *gSum-'Dren Zhabs-Bro*. A little chang is offered three times and drunk fully at the third offering. If the weather is good on that day then it is taken as a sign that the whole year may be peaceful.

During that time, while the sun is rising, in the temple the vajracharya, the umdze (*dBu-mDzad*) music master and one thousand monks read one full Kangyur. Then the monks who had been making the smoke offering return and they all read the gNas-rTan Phyag-mChod-rGyas, the ritual for the sixteen arhat mahastaviras. Buddha ordered them to keep and practise his doctrines so we also request them to do this. This is done according to the ritual system of Dorje Drag.

Then on the high roof, just below the deer and dharmachakra we put the *DGE-BDUN DUNG-'KHOR* and give consecration (*Rab-gNas*). After that all monks go with a volume of the *KANGYUR* or *TENGYUR* (*BSTAN-'GYUR*) or other texts and then they circumambulate the whole monastery once and the main temple three times. Then they put the books back in their correct place and go and sit in their own place and then they read the *BLA-MA MCHOD-PA MCHOG NOR-BU'I PHRENG-BA* and make tsog assembled offerings. If there are some very important or high old monks present then the other monks say, *"brTan-bZhugs"*, *"Long life!"*

The village people get up at about 5 a.m. with the first sunlight. The children say *"bKra-Shis bDe-Legs"*, *"Good wishes!"*, to their mother and she says, *"You all must be well!"*. Then they give her arak, distilled alcohol, and she says, *"Phun-Sum-Tshogs"*, *"May you get plenty of everything!"* This system looks very respectful to the mother but in fact she would have been up some three hours before the children, preparing all the food and making everything ready.

The herders celebrate the new year in much the same way as the villagers. The children say, *"bKra-Shis bDe-Legs"* and the mother replies, *"sKu-Khams bZang"* then the children offer their mother a big pot of milk with butter.

Generally good food is not eaten on the first day. At that time the moon is not visible but we believe it is shining on top of Mt Meru and so this is the gods' new year. Therefore we offer the *Zhal-Zas Tshogs* food offerings, *bSangs* juniper smoke offering and so on.

On the SECOND day of the month all the monks from the house of Nuden Dorje come to the main temple carrying the complete *KANGYUR*. In the smaller hall these texts are then read right through. The *rDo-rJe sLob-dPon* reads the *BKA'-'DUS LHA-BSANG CHEN-MO*. In the high lamas' houses and in the monastery kitchen and in all the villagers' houses, tripe and sheeps' heads are being cooked for the third day. The cooking is done on the second day because we believe that the moon's reflection is then shining on the ocean which means that it is the new year of the naga snake gods, who are also the gods of cooking, but we do not eat these things until the next day.

On the THIRD day of the month all the great lamas of the monastery join the general assembly. All the villagers from nearby request that each year the *KANGYUR* should be read at least once. This third day is the humans' new year since on that day the new moon is visible to us. So then we eat good food and go visiting each other's houses.

The mahavajracharya, with the umdze music master comes into the temple on the third day with the torma (gTor-Ma) assistant, the music master's assistants, the Tsultrim Gekö (Tshul-Khrims dGe-mKod) monks' manager and his assistants and others. Then each monk gets a very large piece of meat and many khapse biscuits and small red potatoes. Then after that Khordong Terchen sends them each a lump of sugar and khapse biscuits as a symbol of their being invited to his house. And the public relations officer tells them, "This is the great lama's food for you."

Then from the FOURTH TO THE SEVENTH day only the general texts are read. That is, the CHOS-sPYOD RAB-GSAL in the morning and the CHOS-sKYONG BsKANG-GSOL prayers of supplication and repair in the afternoon.

From the SEVENTH TO THE FIFTEENTH the old monks who follow Sherab Membar read the sNAR-THANG BKA'-'GYUR and the BsTAN-'GYUR and rNYING-MA rGYUD-'BUM. Then they read the BDE-CAN ZHING-sGRUB for eight days. They practise the BDE-CAN MYUR-LAM and the BDE-CAN sMON-LAM of Raga Asyes to facilitate rebirth in the Pure Land of Amitabha and the vajracharya or abbot gives teachings on this and on Amitabha. At this time only white food [i.e. no meat] is eaten. Traditionally in east Tibet about 99% of the people did not eat chicken, eggs or fish. If the vajracharya is famous and popular many villagers, perhaps one or two thousand, will come to hear the teaching. They sit on the verandah.

From the TENTH TO THE FIFTEENTH day in accordance with the system of Pema Trinle (Padma 'Phrin-Las), some monks read the sGYU-'PHRUL BKA'-MA.

On the THIRTEENTH day some monks practise the 'KHOR-sDE sPYI-TsHANG purifying all of samsara and nirvana of Khordong Gonpo Wangyal ('Khor-gDong mGon-Po dBang-rGyal) at Serlog Gang (gSer-Log sGang), the place where the uncle of Sherab Membar stopped hailstones descending and joined them altogether in a heap by pointing his finger at them.

On the FIFTEENTH, the full moon day, at the end of the bDe-Can-Zhing sGrub the mahavajracharya will give an initiation either from Ratna

Lingpa (*Ratna gLing-Pa*) or the '*Dro-Ba Kun-sGrol* of Rigdzin Godem (*Rig-'Dzin rGod-lDem*), together with the practice of the thousand buddhas. Other monks do many *bDe-Can-Zhing Tshogs* offerings. Organising the butterlamps is the responsibility of the *sTong-mChod gNyer-Pa*, the steward of the thousand offerings. On that day other monks are reading the *Kangyur* and the *sNgags-bSo* from the treasure of Khordong Terchen.

From the **sixteenth to the twenty-fourth** day apart from private practice, only the general daily texts are read.

On the **twenty-fifth** day at the Serkhang yellow house of Nuden Dorje, the Jangter practice of *mKha'-'Gro gSang-Ba Ye-Shes* is read. If some great lama is sick then help will be given to him by means of this practice and also by the associated dakinis' dance.

From the **twenty-sixth to the twenty-eighth** day the general puja texts are read.

On the **twenty-ninth** day the *mKha'-'Gro gSang-Ba Ye-Shes bSu-bZlog* is read, outside if possible, otherwise the *Phur-Pa bZlog-Pa* of Gonpo Wangyal is read.

On **new moon day** the *gSo-sByong* is read and then the *sNgags-Srung* of Rigdzin Tsasum Kundu (*Rig-'Dzin rTsa-gSum Kun-'Dus*).

On the **eighth day of each month** there is the ritual of the Medicine Buddha (*sMan-bLa*, Supreme Healer). All the offering funds for this come each year from the house of Sherab Membar. They send three thousand khal [about 42,000 kilos] of barley each year.

At the **tenth day** rituals performed each month, the *Mang-Ja* or general tea offerings are sponsored by the herders from *Jatami Chen Yu* and *mChog-Tshang*.

On the **fifteenth day of each month** the general tea offering comes from the property of the Khordong Utrul ('*Khor-gDong dBu-sPrul*), which gives two thousand khal of barley per year.

For the *Zhi-'Khro* puja three thousand khal come from the property of Gonpo Wangyal.

The *sNgags-bSo* on no moon day is sponsored by the first *Lha-Brang* of Sherab Membar. They send half the barley in the house, which amounts to some seven thousand khal.

15

Comments on Culture

Culture has three aspects: that which is acquired by participation, the traditional aspects which are adopted, and culture acquired by education.

Regarding the culture acquired by participation, this is the way of behaving which surrounds a child when it is born. It is the 'natural' or 'given' culture of the family. It is what is taken for granted, what seems normal. It is acquired by participation and requires no formal study. It has aspects which are absorbed through participation, for example the dialect of the family, and it has aspects which are revealed through participation, for example the child's own character traits and disposition, generous, selfish and so on.

Within three or four days of a child being born it is shown to its wider family who are happy to have a new member. Those who are not in the family group are indifferent as the child is just another person needing food and clothing. The child cries and this is a sign that it needs help. By the time it has grown to the height of an adult's arm's length, it is able to say, "OM MANI PADME HUNG HRI". It is not necessary to teach a child to say this since it hears it all the time. If a child is happy when it sees a lama or witnesses lama dancing, then, when other people have difficulties and sorrow, that child will also feel sorrow and wish to make the others happy. If somebody has trouble from an enemy then a good child will be sad, a middling child will not respond, and a bad child will say that this is good. This is general village culture transmitted directly and indirectly in thousands of moments of interaction. Some knowledge of good and bad is necessary if one is going to survive in the world. This knowledge can be rigid or flexible depending on how it is acquired.

Regarding traditional culture, each village area in Tibet had its own local culture determining the hairstyles, shoes, clothes and ornaments for men and for women. It was not allowed for individuals to mix up their style of dress. Even when they travelled many thousand kilometers to trade or on pilgrimage they would maintain the dress style of their village. Children take on the dress of the place where they are born. They also maintain the dialect of that area. The villages also have their own system of making offerings during worship and this was maintained from generation to generation. Family connection was maintained by speaking in a friendly manner, by a willingness to assist everyone in the family and by maintaining a good connection with the environment. For example, every day water was taken to the door and three drops were offered to the sky for the Three Jewels.

Regarding culture acquired by education, through parents, teachers and village elders, children learn formal culture through stories and examples. Educational stories were also presented when rituals were performed for sick people. Moreover educational dramas such as those developed by Druptob Thangtong Gyalpo, Drowo Zangmo, Alche Nangsa, Padma Odbar and so on were regularly performed and these dramas showed how good results flowed from good actions and bad results arose from bad actions.

Borrowing

"Who not know anyone not get anything" – for it is not the custom to lend to strangers. However if someone is known well, then if they need money or horses or yaks, they are given whatever is needed. If an animal is to be repaid it is not necessary to give exactly the same horse. If a horse has died then the owner might say that he needed a horse with particular qualities but he is not allowed to exaggerate in this. In these circumstances, if the owner did make a false claim then the whole village will know that he is bad and so he will be shamed.

If items are borrowed for a year then typically if a hundred items are borrowed then one hundred and five should be returned. However there were some greedy businessmen who wanted one hundred and twenty returned on a hundred loaned as the monthly interest rate. There was also a deposit system where you were required to deposit an item worth three times as much as you wanted to borrow. Some lenders were fair-minded but some were shameless. For example, a lender might say he would come at noon on the fifteenth day of the third month to receive his debt but then would not turn up to receive it, or would come late, or would say he had been there when in fact he had not. On the basis of this, lenders would demand more money. Many people did this.

However if a monk does business for a sponsor or to raise funds for the monastery then they had to behave very carefully because they understand that actions have consequences. If a monk does business to make money just for himself then that is terrible work.

Rich and poor

Firstly I say that if from tomorrow for nine to ten years, a house had neither income nor crops, they would still have enough food. In east Tibet there was so much food available that there was no reason for anyone to be hungry. Also, people, be they shepherds or farmers, ate very simple food which was also very healthy and nourishing.

Generally each house had a minimum of fifty to a hundred acres and the richest person might have a thousand acres of land. If farmers were not lazy they could gain at harvest thirty to sixty times the seed they had planted. We also believe that if we are practising virtue then our efforts will be fruitful due to this virtue. Thus, before we commence agricultural activity we make offerings to the land gods, snake gods, water gods, all of whom are under the control of Vajrapani. In the middle of the growing season we make offerings to the Lha Srin De Gye, the eight groups of local spirits, so that they will not make trouble for the crops or cause frost, hail, rust, or landslides. However if they take the offerings and then make hail or cause rust there are specific practices that we would do. For example, in my area, we practised the Green Tara according to Gonpo Wangyal and this brought the crops back to full strength.

At the harvest we always give generously to people who are in retreat even if they are in caves far from our country. Within a month of the harvest coming into the house we perform kangso for reparation and each house also practised the zhitro mandala of peaceful and wrathful deities for one to four days for the sake of the many insects who were killed during the agricultural work. Then later, before planting the next cycle, we do the rituals of the wealth god.

Crops

Our main food is tsampa so we grow barley, both white and blue, to roast and grind. We also have sowa and the thick-skinned rye, yugpo, with which we also make tsampa. Wheat is grown in some places but not in our area which was too cold. Peas are grown. We also grow maize, marmo lotok. It grows tall and sprouts hair which we call ngema, but it does not ripen fully. It is the same with chilli, tomato and sunflowers - flowers appear but no seeds.

Diet

In Tibet we had radish, turnip, spinach, cabbage and potato and they were grown around Lhasa, but in my area we had no interest in them. In general we ate no vegetables. We are like tigers; we eat meat. We also eat tsampa, butter, curds and cheese. Always the same food so there was no difficulty for our body.

In our country we did not make use of bones or old bad meat because we had an excess of food and even had to throw away curds. In the rainy season it was not possible to preserve the milk or to make cheese so much was thrown away. We also grew a very small red potato that was eaten with butter. We did not grow vegetables but grew flowers. We would ignore any vegetables if they grew. After I came to live in Kalimpong I started to eat vegetables. If I told my country people what I ate, they would say, *"Now you have become a cow"*!

Meat

Where did we get meat? Generally from shepherds but also from the village. Why do Buddhists eat meat? Yes, looks very bad but even in the Tibetan Tripitaka you will find no clear restriction placed by the Buddha on eating meat. The Buddha says, *"Kindly don't do it."* Also we avoid killing animals because of the four aspects of karmic accumulation: the basis, which is reification; the intention, which is selfish;

the action, which is hurtful; and the outcome, which is happiness for the one at the expense of the other. Because religious people follow the Tripitaka we do not neglect this instruction and therefore monks do not kill their own meat but are given it by others.

The laypeople, the herders and villagers, would say that killing is not bad because even if one practises not killing, these animals will die anyway within five to ten years.

Firewood

If you were not lazy or old, not blind or disabled, then within five minutes' walk from your house and without much effort you could easily get five days' wood supply. The kitchen stove must always have fire burning in it so that we have hot water available and can make tea whenever we need it. We use hot water for cooking meat or tea and can easily make more if guests come. Did we drink hot water? No, this was only for those who could not digest tea.

Accommodation

Herders live in black tents made from yak hair. These tents can be big or small, from twenty to fifty feet in diameter and five to twelve feet as the height on each side. They were made of strips of wool, each woven one span wide. This narrow weave made them very strong.

Agricultural people have four to five rooms, each with one door and no side windows but just a long hole in the roof for smoke and light which had to be covered over in time of rain. Their doors were useless. Sometimes in the morning I have seen people sleeping surrounded by sheep and dogs. When I asked them, *"Don't you keep the door closed?"*, they said, *"Yes"*, then I asked, *"So where did the sheep come in?"*. They replied, *"Through the door."* We also had thieves. Some stole due to poverty but there were also some rich thieves.

Animals

In my area a poor person would own fifty to a hundred yaks, ten to twenty horses and one to five hundred sheep but rich people would have a thousand horses [*tongta*] and ten thousand dzo and yaks [*trindzo*]. To count the dzo they just show one big black mass when looking down from the hill. A dzo has a yak for a father and a cow for a mother, just as a mule has a horse for a father and a donkey for a mother. They would also own some sheep and goats but it was not the custom of our herders to have many goats.

There were also non-domesticated animals such as the drong, which is like a buffalo but with very long horns, up to five or six feet in length. If they were killed and weighed they would give perhaps fifty quintals of meat, which is similar to an Indian elephant. There is also the kyang, a small mountain horse and gyara[1], gowa[2], shawa[3], nawa[4], tso[5], chiru[6] and kyin[7] – there were many horned animals with cloven feet including musk deer. There were tigers, leopards, bears, tremong[8], forest cats, foxes, wolves, sa[9], yu[10] – many different carnivores.

There were big crows, cha tra ma, chung gong kye, ke chi war, nyu dzang and many other birds.

Also in and near water there were frogs, small and big fish, and sometimes in big rivers there were fish that were even able to block the river - but this is a bad sign!

There were some snakes, small and very dangerous. There were many flying creatures such as butterflies, fireworms and so on but we did not have any honey bees. In our house there were cats, rats, ordinary flies and cloth-eating worms.

Seasons

From the end of the fifth month to late in the sixth month there were six weeks of continuous rain during which you would never see the sun or the sky. Also in Tibet in the eleventh and twelfth months there was a lot of snow and airless weather during which time old people found it difficult to breathe and many would die.

On long journeys it was necessary to cross many rivers and, from the third to the tenth month, because there were few bridges, many detours were necessary and this made the journey very slow. However from the tenth month to the beginning of the third month it was possible to go everywhere quickly because the rivers were frozen. So a journey that took two days in summer could be done in half an hour in winter. For this reason when people travelled for the purposes of culture or meeting others they preferred to do it in winter time.

Eating and drinking

Our tea came from China. We added milk to it and only very rarely did we add butter. In some nearby areas people made a kind of soup with tsampa and strong tea and this would be eaten with cheese, curd and meat. Milk and sweet things were considered to be children's food.

For healthy people, in the morning when they could see the lines in their hands, they would take tea and tsampa, cheese and butter. Then at about 9 a.m. they would have tea and tsampa. At noon they would have tsampa, meat, butter and curds. At 4 p.m., tea and tsampa. At 8 p.m., tea, tsampa, thugpa [soup], meat, curd, cheese. Each village had its own customs regarding food and even each house would have its own practices. Four meals a day was considered essential but five was better. If one was only eating four meals, then the last meal was at 5:30 p.m..

Monks took the same food but those who had taken the full gelong ordination did not eat food that required cutting or chewing after 12 noon.

Sleeping and wakening

Lay people woke at the first sound the cock made. They ate to fill their stomachs and then went outside and came back for lunch at 2 pm. They did not work after this and slept immediately after dinner.

Monks also woke at cockcrow. They would recite scriptures and practise meditation. They would continue this throughout the whole day following the pattern of their monastery and then sleep after dinner and the completion of their required daily recitations. Young monks go to sleep early and old monks can go to sleep later. However nobody sleeps after 4.30 to 5 a.m. when the sky is shining. That is the village people's view and the village monks' practice, however monastery monks have a different idea.

NOTES

[1] Gyara, a type of goat-antelope, Capricornis sumatraensis.

[2] Gowa, Tibetan gazelle, Procapra picticuadata.

[3] McNeil's Deer, Cervus elaphus macneilli.

[4] Nawa, Blue-sheep or bharal, Pseudois nayaur.

[5] Tso, another type of gazelle.

[6] Chiru, Tibetan antelope with very long horns, Pantholops hodgsoni.

[7] Kyin, Ibex, Capra ibex.

[8] Tremong, Tibetan brown bear, Ursus arctos pruinosus.

[9] Sa, Snow leopard, Panthera uncia.

[10] Yu, lynx.

16

Rigdzin Godem and Sikkim

There are three excellent incarnations who are the highest treasure revealers (*gTer-sTon*), each having the blessings of Padmasambhava's Body, Speech and Mind. The sun-like Terton who is the incarnation of the Guru's Body is Ngadag Nyang Nyima Odzer (*mNga'-lDag Nyang Nyi-Ma 'Od-Zer*). The moon-like Terton who is the incarnation of the Guru's Speech is Guru Chokyi Wangchuk (*Guru Chos-Kyi dBang-Phyug*). The Terton who is like a wish-fulfilling gem, the incarnation of the Guru's Mind, is Rigdzin Gokyi Dem Truchen (*Rig-'Dzin rGod-Kyi lDem-'Phru-Can*).

Here we are concerned with the Mind incarnation, Rigdzin Gokyi Dem Truchen, known as Rigdzin Godem. He was born on the tenth day of the first month of the water-ox year in the northern part of Tibet, at the village of Toryor Nepo (*Thor-Yor Nas-Po*), in front of the east side of the hill called Riwo Trabzang (*Ri-Bo bKra-bZang*). His father, Lopon Dudul (*sLob-dPon bDud-'Dul*), belonged to the Hor people; his mother was Jochem Sonam Khyedren (*Jo-lCam bSod-Nams Khye-'Dren*) and he was named Ngodrub Gyaltsen (*dNgos-Grub rGyal-mTshan*).

The text '*KHRUNGS-RABS sGRON-MA rNAM-gSUM* says, "*His head is large with a high dome as the sign that his view and understanding are very high and difficult to fathom. He has a mole at the brahmaranda on the crown of his head, the sign that his wisdom door is open."* Thus it lists his symbolic characteristics.

Also the text *sNYING-THIG MAN-NGAG DON-BDUN* which is a treasure (gTer) of Rigdzin Godem himself, says, *"Born in the water-ox year he possesses the symbol of a mole, and as a sign of having been blessed by Padmasambhava, vulture feathers come twice on the crown of his head."*

Thus at the age of twelve, three vulture's feathers appeared at the crown of his head and when he was twenty-four, two more vulture's feathers appeared so that he had five in all.

At the age of twenty-five he found the naga's Man-Shel jewel at the spring called Dutsi Chumig (*bDud-rTsi'i Chu-Mig*). He showed it to Zangpo Dragpa (*bZang-Po Grags-Pa*) who stayed in the hermitage called Manglam Ritro (*Mang-Lam Ri-Khrod*).   With the latter's guidance, on the eighth day of the snake month of the fire-horse year, when he was twenty-nine years of age, from the three stone pillars of white *'Dzeng* rock near the top of Riwo Trabzang he took out the keys or guides to three great treasures (*gTer*) and one hundred small treasures (*gTer*) and he deposited there some treasure replacements (*gTer-Tshab*).

At about nine in the evening on the fourth day of the sheep month of that same year, at the cave of Zangzang Lhadrag (*Zang-Zang Lha-Brag*) on the ridge of Riwo Trabzang which looks like a heap of dangerous snakes, Rigdzin Godem took out the maroon leather treasure casket[1] that was made by three people whose names each ended in Gon (*mGon*). This casket was divided into one central and four side compartments, and from these he took out the great profound treasures (*gTer*) known as the 'five treasures', Dzonga (*mDzod-lNga*). To describe them briefly, in the centre is the *sNying-mDzod sMug-Po*, the maroon coloured heart treasury.   At the east is the *Dung-mDzod dKar-Po*, the white coloured conch treasury.   At the south is the *gSer-mDzod Ser-Po*, the yellow coloured golden treasury.   At the west is the *Zangs-mDzod dMar-Po*, the red coloured copper treasury.   At the north is the *lCags-mDzod Nag-Po*, the black coloured iron treasury. These treasuries contain the texts on *BLA-SGRUB; RDZOG-CHEN DGONGS-PA ZANG-THAL* and *KA-DAG; RTSA-RLUNG PHAG-MO ZAB-RGYAS; THUGS-SGRUB GSANG-SGRUB DRAG-PO RTSAL* among others. Rigdzin Godem wrote out more than five hundred texts on the basis of these core texts.

In general, the profound Ter (*gTer*) treasures are the sole method for bringing happiness to Tibet and other countries now and in future. In particular these Jang Ter (*Byang-gTer*) are the ones which promote the Dharma, prevent war, stop epidemics, pacify inner strife, control demons, nourish the state and control dangerous diseases, for they contain everything necessary to benefit beings.

These doctrines also contain the key or guide to many places and especially the seven great secret holy places. For these reasons the Jang Ter is famous everywhere as 'The one Ter (*gTer, treasure*) which is like a protective minister in providing benefit for the whole of Tibet.'

At the end of his life Rigdzin Godem went to Sikkim (*'Bras-Mo gShongs*) and opened the way to the holy places[2]. He became the Guru of Chogdrub De (*mChog-sGrub-sDe*) the King of Gung-Thang and this brought happiness to the people of Tibet.

Then finally, having performed many such deeds, at the age of seventy-two years with many amazing signs he merged his mind into the all-encompassing space of the dharmadhātu. Thus he greatly benefited both sentient beings and the dharma.

From Ladakh in the west to *Dar-rTse mDo* [Tachienlu] near the Chinese border, and from the Mongolian lands in the north to the Sikkim of former times in the south, there have been many lineage holders of the Jangter and now they may also spread to western countries.

When Rigdzin Godem Truchen (*Rig-'Dzin rGod-lDem 'Phru-Can*) was opening the way to the holy places of Sikkim he made this prayer:

> "*Body, Speech, Mind. Great Teacher, grant me all true attainments. Although I know worldly appearances to be illusory, there still arises grasping at these bewildering appearances as being something inherently real. My afflictions and their subtle traces are not yet finished. Please bless me by cutting the root of all hopes and desires.*
>
> *Body, Speech, Mind. Great Teacher, grant me all true attainments. Towards the impermanent manifestations of the bad actions of this debased period, renunciation arises and I discard the objects of my hopes and desires. Yet later on I am troubled by the suffering of desire for the objects of my daily use. Please bless me by cutting the root of desire and craving.*

Body, Speech, Mind. Great Teacher, grant me all true attainments. Great methods for clearing away the afflictions of the three poisons have been spoken by the Jinas in many teachings, yet I very strongly go under the power of the subtle karmic traces that are so difficult to abandon. Please bless me by cutting the root of bad actions.

Body, Speech, Mind. Great Teacher, grant me all true attainments. Outer causal situations, inner causal situations, and suddenly occurring causal situations all arise from the root of belief in duality. I now know this, yet I am not free from the power of Mara's obstacles. Please bless me that my mind may arise nakedly.

Body, Speech, Mind. Great Teacher, grant me all true attainments. Please bless me with freedom from the fetter of belief in duality. Mind itself is unmade, coming easily in its own mode. It is not made by the good deeds and qualities of the Buddhas, and it is not bound by the prison of sinking, fogginess and wavering. With the brilliant, radiant, natural shining light of awareness, dharmata's vast mother and child will meet.

So not being made stupid by the bad friends of lazy, relaxed situations, I will strongly and lovingly protect the good house of sunyata, and by that, dharmata mother and child will quickly meet.

Then, from that time on, I must strongly act for the benefit of those moving in samsara. I must perform the deeds of a Bodhisattva. I must accomplish a great wave of virtue for the benefit of others. I must gain the effective power to upturn and empty samsara."

NOTES

[1] The casket is one cubit high, shaped like a jewel and with a maximum circumference of one full arm span.

[2] It had previously been a hidden and unknown land.

DEDICATION

If there is any merit in this book, we dedicate it to all sentient beings
And if there is none, may it dissolve in its own empty nature.

ཕན་པར་བསམས་པ་ཙམ་གྱིས་ཀྱང་།
སངས་རྒྱས་མཆོད་ལས་ཁྱད་འཕགས་ན།
སེམས་ཅན་མ་ལུས་ཐམས་ཅད་ཀྱི།
བདེ་དོན་བརྩོན་པ་སྨོས་ཅི་དགོས།།

When merely the thought of helping others
Is more excellent than the worship of all the Buddhas
It is unnecessary even to mention the greatness of striving
For the happiness of all beings without exception.

[From the Bodhicharyavatara by Shantideva]

Bibliography

Low J. *SIMPLY BEING: TEXTS IN THE DZOGCHEN TRADITION*, 3rd ed., (CPI Antony Rowe, November 2010)

Lama, C.R. and Low, J. *RADIANT ASPIRATION: THE BUTTERLAMP PRAYER LAMP OF ASPIRATION*, (Simply Being, July 2011)

Low, J. *BEING GURU RINPOCHE: A COMMENTARY ON NUDEN DORJE'S TERMA, VIDYADHARA GURU SADHANA*, (Trafford, Canada, 2006)

Low, J. *BEING RIGHT HERE: THE MIRROR OF CLEAR MEANING*, (Shambala Publications, 2004)

Lama, C.R. And Low, J. R. *THE SEVEN CHAPTERS OF PRAYER, AS TAUGHT BY PADMASAMBHAVA OF URGYEN, KNOWN IN TIBETAN AS LE'U BDUN MA*, (edition khordong, 2008)

Dudjom Rinpoche, Jikdrel Yeshe Dorje. Dorje, G. (Tr and Ed). *THE NYINGMA SCHOOL OF TIBETAN BUDDHISM: ITS FUNDAMENTALS AND HISTORY*, (Wisdom Publications, Boston, 1991)

www.ingramcontent.com/pod-product-compliance
Lightning Source LLC
Chambersburg PA
CBHW060317100426
42812CB00003B/804

* 9 7 8 0 9 5 6 9 2 3 9 2 9 *